What's Gaby Cooking

TAKE IT
EASY

RECIPES FOR ZERO STRESS DELICIOUSNESS

Editor: Holly Dolce
Designer: Claudia Wu
Design Manager: Danielle Youngsmith
Managing Editor: Annalea Manalili
Production Manager: Kathleen Gaffney

Library of Congress Control Number: 2022932222

ISBN: 978-1-4197-5886-7
eISBN: 978-1-64700-533-7

Text copyright © 2022 Gaby Dalkin
Photographs copyright © 2022 Matt Armendariz

Cover © 2022 Abrams

Printed and bound in China
10 9 8 7 6 5 4 3 2 1

Abrams books are available at special discounts when purchased in quantity
for premiums and promotions as well as fundraising or educational use.
Special editions can also be created to specification. For details, contact
specialsales@abramsbooks.com or the address below.

Abrams® is a registered trademark of Harry N. Abrams, Inc.

ABRAMS The Art of Books
195 Broadway, New York, NY 10007
abramsbooks.com

What's Gaby Cooking

TAKE IT EASY

RECIPES FOR ZERO STRESS DELICIOUSNESS

Gaby Dalkin

PHOTOGRAPHY BY MATT ARMENDARIZ

Abrams, New York

What's Inside

Introduction

From the time I first started writing cookbooks about three lifetimes ago (seriously, how has it been nine years since my first book?), my number one goal has always been to give my readers a taste of the good life. I've wanted all of you, whether you are reading my books or following me on social media, to be able to plug into a way of living that brings you more: more getting together with friends, more seeing the world through the flavors on your plate, more sunshine, more of the things that make you happy, and of course, more delicious meals. All of that started with encouraging you to get into the kitchen. You just had to find a recipe that inspired you, grab the freshest ingredients possible, and treat yourself to a home-cooked meal—then pour yourself a Negroni spritz while you kicked back and enjoyed the fruits of your labor. And I still stand by that because it's how I have been cooking at home too.

Then two huge things happened in my life that shifted the way I think about food. The first was the birth of my daughter, Poppy. Suddenly I had somewhere I'd much rather be than in the kitchen—which is really saying something considering my happy place is organizing my pantry and dreaming up new dishes to cook for pretty much every meal. But the reality is, my life has changed and so has my cooking. Granted, I still want the same mega flavors that I'm always after, but I don't want to spend a lot of time building them. I still want the same hearty, filling, nourishing dishes that are my longtime loves and go-tos, but I want them to come together even more quickly. We're talking less babysitting pots, and more babysitting Poppy, if you know what I mean. So, I started thinking about ingredients that can pop on their own without necessarily needing a lot of hand-holding, and dishes that shine in their simplicity—things like Lemon

Feta Herby Orzo (page 135), Sausage Sheet Pan Supper (page 57), and Summer Pasta with Burst Sun Golds (page 85).

The other major life-altering event—though in a very, very, very different way—was 2020. I don't think I need to remind you about what that hot mess of a year was all about, but I will say that it made me learn some pretty significant things about myself: how important it is to connect with other people, how special it is to have others sharing and laughing around my table, and how much I genuinely love feeding my friends and family. I mean, my husband, Thomas, is my favorite person in the world (besides Poppy), but there are only so many cacio e pepe pizzas that I can make for just the two of us. So, when life started to return to normal and it was once again safe to get together, it was like the floodgates opened—I couldn't wait to see everyone. And not just that, feed everyone. But this time around felt different. Whereas in the past I might have been excited to take painstaking care over an impressively involved menu, now

I wanted to give as much of my undivided attention as possible to my guests—not the food. Add a baby into the mix, and this girl definitely doesn't have 1,348,954 hours to prep. No, now I want to reach for dishes that come together quickly, shine their brightest at room temperature (aka, make-ahead-then-forget-all-about-them kinda deals), and lend themselves to all the dipping, picking, and nibbling that happens in between catching up on all the scoop. Dishes like Crab Cake Salad (page 69), Baja fish tacos (page 96), BLT pizza (page 139), and Skillet Upside-Down Peach Cake (page 196). Because if there's one thing I now know for sure, it's that coming together isn't about what's on the table. It's about who is at it. And I realize that if I'm going to enjoy myself and soak up every precious minute with the people who matter most to me, then I need to loosen up a little bit in the kitchen.

But that by no stretch means that I take my food any less seriously. The opposite is true—I made it my mission to develop a book's worth of recipes that do all the hard work for you. Because these days, taking it easy is my jam. Or more accurately, taking it easy is my Basil Vinaigrette (page 235). I'm all about food that fits real, everyday life and not the other way around. And these are the recipes to make that happen. We're talking staring-at-the-fridge-at-seven-p.m.-trying-to-figure-out-what's-for-dinner, one-pan, one-serving-bowl, one-grocery-store kind of dishes that will also be perfectly suitable for company, whether it's a Sunday barbecue or a polished but laid-back lunch. (I have the perfect menu for you, one with all the Italy vibes.) These chapters are packed full of fridge-staple dressings, clutch sauces for lazy last-minute meals, simple mains, and obviously—because it's me we're talking about—big, fresh salads that are easy to whip up, plus effortless yet rich-because-you're-in-your-sweatpants-anyway desserts. I also threw in some signature dishes—or the Ultimates, as I like to call them—that, once you master them, you could make with your eyes closed and still look like a total boss. Oh, and there's the Perfect Banana Bread (page 23). Because if there's

one good thing to come out of a global pandemic, it might as well be the most delicious thing ever.

Even though this book is staying true to my What's Gaby Cooking roots—simple, fresh, flavorful food that you can feel really good about eating—I'd really like to think of it as a celebration of where we are now and the lessons we've all learned after so much time apart. I know for me, these past couple years have really brought home how important it is to be surrounded by people who lift me up (like my WGC community!), to not take myself too seriously, and to work hard and leisure harder. This is a true TYM (Treat Yourself Moment). Give yourself permission to kick back, relax, and make some really good food without breaking a sweat. Do yourself a favor—crack open this book, pour yourself a glass of rosé, throw together a little tasty something (Soft Scramble Toast? BBQ chicken chopped salad? Tri-tip sandwich? Nutella pie?), and Take. It. Easy. You earned it.

XO, Gaby

Kick-Start the Day

Yes, this book is all about taking it easy, but that does not mean selling yourself short when it comes to breakfast. I know it seems so much easier to either skip it or reach for something packaged. But be honest—how do you feel when eleven a.m. rolls around and you're hangry/brain foggy/ running on empty? That's why no matter how tight for time I am, I will always have breakfast at the top of my to-do list as one of my self-care essentials. Luckily, I've perfected the art of quick, satisfying morning meals that can be taken on the go, in addition to more impressive spreads for when you're entertaining or feeling like you deserve a more decadent brunch. (Spoiler alert: You do.) From Cacio e Pepe Soft Scramble to cheesy omelets, I've got all the egg dishes you could want. There are the most perfect hash browns known to man. Or you can get baking with Perfect Banana Bread and Coconut French Toast Bread Pudding for some tropical inspo. And let's just say that Alex's Chilaquiles Breakfast Nachos will pretty much change your life.

Page 28:
Broccoli + Leek Spanish-ish Omelet

Cacio e Pepe
Soft Scramble

My favorite style of pasta meets my favorite way to make eggs.
As always, I say the more Pecorino and black pepper, the better. End of story.

Serves 2

4 large eggs
Kosher salt
1 teaspoon freshly cracked black
    pepper, plus more for serving
1 tablespoon unsalted butter
¼ cup (25 g) freshly grated Pecorino
    Romano or Parmesan cheese

In a medium bowl, crack the eggs and whisk together with a pinch of salt and the pepper until smooth. In a large nonstick skillet, melt the butter over medium-low heat. Once it is bubbling, carefully pour the eggs into the hot pan. Slowly drag a spatula along the bottom of the pan, allowing the eggs to cook slowly and evenly. Add the cheese while the eggs are still runny and continue to slowly cook.

Once the eggs are almost set on the surface but still look slightly runny, season them with additional salt and pepper depending on your preferences and top with more shredded cheese. Remove the eggs from the heat and let the residual heat from the pan finish cooking them. They should still look very soft. Serve immediately.

Omelet for Two

There is no quicker dish to come together than eggs, and it doesn't get more classic than an omelet stuffed with cheese and fresh herbs. I figured I'd make things a little more interesting by cranking this up to jumbo-size for two, but the technique is still standard operating procedure and can be used for any number of eggs.

In a medium bowl, whisk together the eggs and heavy cream. Season with 1 teaspoon salt and ½ teaspoon pepper.

In a 10-inch (25 cm) nonstick fry pan over medium heat, melt the butter, tilting the pan to cover the bottom evenly.

Once the butter is foaming, pour in the egg mixture. As the eggs begin to set around the edge of the skillet, use a rubber spatula to gently push the cooked portions toward the center of the skillet. Lift the skillet to tilt and rotate, allowing the uncooked eggs to flow into empty spaces. If the eggs begin to cook too fast, reduce heat to medium-low.

When the eggs are almost set on the surface but still look slightly runny, cover with ½ cup (55 g) of the cheese and the chives. Cover the skillet with a lid and let cook for 30 seconds.

Remove the lid and carefully slip a rubber spatula under one side of the eggs and flip to fold the omelet in half. Sprinkle it with the remaining ¼ cup (30 g) cheese.

Cover the skillet and continue to cook for 1 minute until the cheese is really melty. Garnish with chives, dill, and flaky salt. Serve immediately.

Serves 2

4 large eggs
2 tablespoons heavy cream
Kosher salt and freshly ground black pepper
1 tablespoon unsalted butter
½ cup (55 g) plus ¼ cup (30 g) freshly shredded Fontina or Cheddar cheese
1 tablespoon minced chives, plus more for garnish
Chopped fresh dill, for garnish
Flaky salt, for serving

The Crispiest
Hash Browns

Sorry, guys. I ate them all. No more hash browns here. That's it. Because when I say that these are a life-altering borderline religious experience hash brown situation, I mean it. They're cheesy, salty, and potato chip-crispy (none of those sad, soggy hash browns here). And they are big and substantial like a latke, because big and substantial is how potato consumption should be. All that's left to do is serve with a generous amount of ketchup.

Serves 4
(or 1 if you are a monster like me)

1½ pounds (680 g) russet potatoes, peeled
½ cup (120 ml) canola oil, plus more as needed
Kosher salt and freshly ground black pepper
Pinch cayenne pepper
2 teaspoons granulated garlic
½ cup (50 g) freshly grated Parmesan cheese
Homemade Ketchup (page 230)

Fill a large bowl with cold water. Using the largest holes on a box grater, shred the peeled potatoes and transfer immediately to the water to avoid browning. Stir the potatoes to release some of their starch and then let them sit in the water for 20 minutes. Stir again, then strain and rinse with cold water to remove the remaining starch.

Transfer the potatoes to a large, thin kitchen towel. Gather the towel ends together, then squeeze as much liquid as possible out of the potatoes. Open the towel, toss the potatoes slightly to loosen, then repeat the process at least two more times. You want the potatoes to be as dry as possible.

Transfer the potatoes to a dry bowl and toss with 2 teaspoons salt, ½ teaspoon black pepper, a small to medium pinch of cayenne pepper depending on desired spice level, and the granulated garlic.

In a large skillet over medium-high heat, warm ¼ cup (60 ml) of the oil until it is just beginning to smoke. Add half of the potatoes and spread into an even layer, pressing them into the oil to create one flat, lacy pancake. Cook until deep golden brown, about 5 minutes. If the potatoes begin to look dry, add another tablespoon or two of oil.

Sprinkle the potatoes with half of the cheese and cook for 30 seconds. Flip the potatoes and continue to cook, breaking them up slightly with a wooden spoon. Continue to cook until deep golden brown and crispy, about 4 minutes longer.

Transfer to a plate lined with a paper towel and sprinkle with salt. Warm the remaining ¼ cup (60 ml) oil in the pan and cook the rest of the potatoes as described above, adding the remaining cheese after the potoatoes are deep golden brown. Serve with homemade ketchup.

Perfect
Banana Bread

I've been attempting to make the ultimate banana bread for years, trying to nail the ideal loaf that's perfectly firm, doesn't collapse in the middle, and is packed with banana-y flavor. Well, it may have taken a global pandemic to do it, but consider it done. The secret, I found, is folding in sour cream, which makes the bread extra tender and moist (I'm sorry, Dagny, I love you) while giving it just the right amount of tang. Serve yourself a slab with a fat dollop of butter as breakfast or a snack, preferably with coffee.

Preheat the oven to 350°F (175°C). Grease an 8 by 4 by 2½-inch (20 by 10 by 6 cm) loaf pan with nonstick cooking spray and line with parchment paper, leaving at least 2 inches (5 cm) overhang on either side.

In a medium bowl, whisk together the flour, baking soda, baking powder, salt, and cinnamon.

In the bowl of a stand mixer, beat together the butter and brown sugar on medium-high speed until light and fluffy, about 3 minutes.

Add the sour cream and eggs, beating until combined and scraping down the sides of the bowl as needed.

Reduce the speed to low and add the flour mixture, beating until just combined. Scrape down the sides of the bowl, then beat in 3 of the bananas until the batter is smooth.

Using a rubber spatula, gently fold in the remaining 2 bananas, keeping some larger pieces intact.

Transfer the batter to the prepared pan and smooth the top.

Bake until a toothpick inserted in the center comes out clean, 65 to 70 minutes. Allow to cool in the pan for 30 minutes, then use the parchment to lift the banana bread out of the pan.

Slice to serve warm with salted butter or continue to cool to room temperature.

Makes 1 loaf; serves 8

1½ cups (190 g) all-purpose flour
1 teaspoon baking soda
1 teaspoon baking powder
1½ teaspoons kosher salt
2½ teaspoons ground cinnamon
5 tablespoons unsalted butter, at room temperature
1 cup (220 g) packed dark brown sugar
⅓ cup (75 ml) plus 3 tablespoons sour cream
2 large eggs
5 large very ripe bananas
Softened lightly salted butter, for serving

Coconut

French Toast Bread Pudding

One of my favorite things to do is travel, so lately I've been nonstop daydreaming about all the vacations that I plan to take as soon as I'm able to. This tropical-inspired breakfast gives me all the island vibes, making me feel like I'm beachside in Hawaii. It started out as a more traditional French toast, but then it became a bread pudding drizzled with brown butter maple syrup, and life just got that much better.

Serves 6

6 large eggs
1 (13½-ounce/400 ml) can full-fat
  coconut milk, shaken
¼ cup (60 ml) heavy cream
¼ cup (50 g) granulated sugar
2 teaspoons vanilla bean paste
  or vanilla extract
2 teaspoons ground cinnamon
½ teaspoon kosher salt
½ teaspoon coconut extract
  (optional)
1½ pounds (680 g) challah,
  cut into 1½-inch (4 cm) cubes
  (roughly 1 large loaf)
12 ounces (340 g) shredded
  sweetened coconut, lightly toasted
¼ cup (60 ml) unsalted butter,
  plus more for the baking dish
½ cup (120 ml) maple syrup,
  plus more for serving
Strawberries, halved, for serving
  (optional)
Crushed macadamia nuts, for garnish
  (optional)

Preheat the oven to 350°F (175°C).

In a large shallow bowl, whisk the eggs. Add the coconut milk, heavy cream, sugar, vanilla, cinnamon, and salt and whisk. If using, add the coconut extract. Add the cubed bread and three-quarters of the toasted coconut and toss to combine. Let sit for an hour.

Grease a 9 by 13-inch (23 by 33 cm) baking dish with butter.

Transfer the cubed bread mixture to the baking dish and bake for 1 hour 15 minutes.

To make the brown butter maple syrup, melt the butter in a pan over medium-low heat until it is lightly browned, then stir the toasty brown butter together with the maple syrup.

Once the pudding is out of the oven, drizzle it with brown butter maple syrup. Serve with the extra maple syrup on the side and top with macadamia nuts and strawberries (if using). Top with toasted coconut and serve warm.

Breakfast Nachos

If chilaquiles and nachos ever had a fling, this dish would be their love child. It combines the smothered-in-sauce base of chilaquiles (in this case a next-level combo of salsa, black beans, and chorizo) with the best part of nachos: the toppings! Here we're loading them up with cheese, eggs (fried or scrambled, your call), and all the Tex-Mex fixings. Also, breakfast beer is totally a thing and completely called for here. Get on board.

Preheat the broiler to high with the rack set in the upper third of the oven.

To make the chilaquiles: In a large skillet over medium-high heat, cook the chorizo until it has loosened and the fat has rendered, stirring occasionally, about 5 minutes. Add the onion and cook until softened, about 7 minutes.

Add the salsa and the entire can of black beans (liquid included), then season with salt and black pepper. Bring to a boil over medium heat, then reduce heat to medium-low and simmer until reduced slightly, about 5 minutes.

Add the chips and toss to coat in the sauce, being careful not to break the chips.

Sprinkle with the cheese and transfer to the oven. Broil until the cheese is melted and bubbly and the exposed chips are crisped, about 2 minutes.

Top with the eggs, pickled or fresh jalapeños (or a combination), Fresno peppers, avocado, sour cream, and cilantro. Serve immediately.

Serves 4

FOR THE CHILAQUILES:

9 ounces (255 g) chorizo

1 large yellow onion, thinly sliced

⅔ cup (165 ml) Chipotle Salsa (page 234)

1 (15-ounce/430 g) can black beans, undrained

Kosher salt and freshly ground black pepper

1 (10 to 12-ounce/280 to 340 g) bag thick tortilla chips

1½ cups (165 g) Mexican blend shredded cheese

FOR THE TOPPING:

3 to 4 large eggs, scrambled or fried

¼ cup (60 g) pickled and/or fresh sliced jalapeños

1 Fresno pepper, thinly sliced

1 to 2 avocados, diced

½ cup (60 ml) sour cream

Fresh cilantro, leaves torn into small pieces

Broccoli + Leek *Spanish-ish* Omelet

If you're feeding a crowd—whether it's guests or your crew at home— then this is the way to do it. You could say that it's my take on a Spanish tortilla, but it's ultimately just a super tasty eggy, potato-y, veg-y dish that's like eggs and sides all in one and comes together in minutes.

Serves 8-10

1 cup (240 ml) plus ¼ cup (60 ml) extra-virgin olive oil, plus more for serving

3 Yukon gold potatoes (1¾ pounds/ 800 g), sliced on a mandolin into ¼-inch (6 mm) slices

½ onion, thinly sliced

1 large leek, thinly sliced into rings

1½ cups (135 g) broccoli florets (from 1 small head broccoli), chopped

Kosher salt and freshly ground black pepper

8 eggs, whisked

2 teaspoons paprika

Sour cream, for serving

Flake salt, for serving

Fresh herbs (basil, dill, chives, parsley), for serving

In a large (12-inch/30.5 cm) nonstick skillet over medium high heat, warm 1 cup (240 ml) of the oil.

Add the potatoes, onion, leek, broccoli, and 1½ tablespoons kosher salt and stir to coat in the oil. Then pour the remaining ¼ cup (60 ml) the oil over the top. The skillet will seem too full, but the vegetables will shrink as they cook.

Once the oil begins to simmer vigorously, reduce the heat to medium-low and cook, stirring often, until the potatoes are fork tender, about 25 minutes. Be careful not to break the potatoes while you stir.

Carefully transfer the mixture to a large bowl. Strain all but 4 tablespoons of the oil to a heat-proof bowl. Use a paper towel or pastry brush to spread the 4 tablespoons of oil all over the bottom and sides of the pan. Discard remaining oil. Let cool for 5 minutes.

Season the eggs with the paprika, 1 teaspoon kosher salt, and 1 teaspoon freshly ground black pepper, then add to the bowl with the potatoes and carefully stir to coat.

Return the oiled skillet to medium-high heat. Add the potato and egg mixture, stirring occasionally and gently spreading it into an even layer, being careful to keep the potatoes intact and distributing the broccoli, leeks, and onion evenly.

Cook until the eggs are beginning to set, about 4 minutes, then reduce heat to medium-low. Continue to cook until the eggs are slightly puffed and just about cooked through, shaking the pan occasionally to prevent sticking, 12 to 15 minutes. If the eggs stick to the edges, use a small offset spatula or knife to loosen.

Meanwhile, preheat the broiler to high with the rack set in the upper third of the oven.

Transfer the skillet to the oven rack and broil until the omelet is fully set on the top, about 3 minutes. Remove from the oven and allow to cool for about 10 minutes, then invert onto a large platter or plate. Allow to cool further, about 10 minutes, then dollop with a generous scoop of sour cream, a sprinkle of flaky salt, fresh herbs, and a drizzle of oil.

Huevos Rancheros

I already knew that I was a huge fan of this traditional Mexican dish, but when I added refried black beans (versus pinto) and mixed them with whole black beans, I got an even richer flavor and better texture. Needless to say, it's now reached full obsession status. It's one of those great recipes that feeds a lot of people with minimal time and effort. Just add breakfast margaritas. Yes, they're a thing (like breakfast beers). Yes, you have my permission.

In a large nonstick skillet over medium-low heat, combine the refried beans, black beans with half the liquid, and salsa. Bring to a simmer and cook until the mixture has thickened and is heated through, about 10 minutes. Season with salt and a squeeze of fresh lime juice.

Turn on a burner to medium-high heat and hold one tortilla at a time with tongs over the flame until lightly charred. If you have an electric stove, warm the tortillas in the microwave for 20 to 30 seconds, until soft. Transfer to a sheet of foil and cover to keep warm while you prepare the rest.

For each serving, top two tortillas with the bean and salsa mixture, then top with a fried egg, a sprinkle of cotija cheese, a dollop of sour cream, hot sauce, avocado, and cilantro. Serve immediately.

Serves 4

1 (16-ounce/454 g) can refried black beans

1 (15-ounce/430 g) can black beans, drained of half the liquid

1 cup (240 ml) Chipotle Salsa (page 234), plus more for serving

Kosher salt

1 squeeze fresh lime juice

8 (6-inch/15 cm) flour or corn tortillas

4 large eggs, fried

4 ounces (115 g) cotija cheese, crumbled

Sour cream, for serving

Hot sauce, for serving

Avocado, sliced, for serving

Fresh cilantro, roughly chopped, for serving

Belle's Baklava Granola

This dish is a double-whammy inspiration. I first got the idea thanks to Souvla in San Francisco, one of my favorite fast-casual restaurants that is an absolute must-go anytime I'm in the city. The one thing I look forward to ordering every single time is their Greek frozen yogurt with baklava, a spiced, nutty, honey-soaked pastry. But the idea to take those flavors and flip the script and make them breakfast? That's all thanks to my friend Belle, one of the few people who cooks for me (such a treat!) and who I love dearly. I go for a big bowl heaped with Greek yogurt and tons of honey.

Makes 5 cups (610 g)

3½ cups (315 g) rolled oats
3 tablespoons dark brown sugar
1 tablespoon ground cinnamon
½ teaspoon ground allspice
1 teaspoon kosher salt
½ cup (120 ml) honey, plus tons
 more for serving
½ cup (120 ml) extra-virgin olive oil
1 tablespoon vanilla extract
1½ cups (180 g) chopped walnuts
1 cup (115 g) chopped pistachios
Greek yogurt, for serving

Place a rack in the upper third of the oven and preheat the oven to 325°F (165°C).

Line a rimmed sheet pan with parchment paper and set aside. In a large bowl toss together the oats, brown sugar, cinnamon, allspice, and salt.

In a small saucepan over low heat, add the honey, oil, and vanilla and stir until evenly combined. Allow to cool for 5 minutes, then pour over the oat mixture and stir. Toss in the walnuts and pistachios and stir again to combine.

Spread into an even layer across the prepared sheet pan. Bake for 35 to 40 minutes, tossing every 10 to 12 minutes to ensure even browning. Bake until golden brown. The granola will come out seemingly soggy but will crisp as it cools.

Serve with the yogurt, and top with an extra honey drizzle.

Soft Scramble Toast

I'll see your boring, plain toast and raise you crisped bread topped
with a soft scramble, salty prosciutto, and plenty of freshly grated Parm.
I can't tell if this is an open-faced breakfast sandwich or an affirmation
that everything's going to be okay.

In a medium nonstick skillet over low heat, melt the butter.

Add the eggs and cook until softly scrambled, stirring constantly. Fold in the
cheese and season with salt and pepper.

Meanwhile, toast the bread in a toaster and spread with butter.

In a small bowl, toss the arugula with the oil, lemon zest, Parmesan, and some
salt and black pepper.

Place the soft scrambled eggs on the toast and top with the arugula,
prosciutto, and crushed red pepper.

Serves 1

FOR THE SOFT SCRAMBLE:
1 tablespoon unsalted butter
2 large eggs, whisked
¼ cup (25 g) freshly grated
    Parmesan cheese
Kosher salt and freshly ground
    black pepper

FOR THE TOAST:
1 (1-inch/2.5 cm) thick slice
    sourdough
1 tablespoon unsalted butter

FOR THE TOPPING:
¼ cup (5 g) packed arugula
Drizzle extra-virgin olive oil
½ teaspoon freshly grated lemon zest
2 tablespoons freshly grated
    Parmesan cheese, plus more
    for serving
Kosher salt and freshly ground
    black pepper
1½ ounces (40 g) thinly sliced
    Prosciutto (about 3 slices)
Crushed red pepper

Geri's
Farm Breakfast

This breezy breakfast is inspired by my effortlessly chic friend Geri who lives on an incredible ranch in Santa Ynez, which is exactly 125 miles north of my house in Los Angeles (not that I am counting). It's equal parts delicious and minimalist and is for sure going to get your day started on the right foot.

Serves 1

FOR THE EVERYTHING SEASONING:

2 tablespoons white sesame seeds
1½ tablespoons black sesame seeds
1½ tablespoons dried minced onions
1½ tablespoons dried minced garlic
1 tablespoon flaky salt or kosher salt
1½ teaspoons poppy seeds

FOR THE BREAKFAST:

1 tomato, sliced, or a handful of
  cherry tomatoes, halved
½ avocado, sliced
Soft scrambled eggs (see page 35)
Drizzle of extra-virgin olive oil
1 tablespoon Everything Seasoning
  (recipe above)

TO MAKE THE EVERYTHING SEASONING: Combine the white and black sesame seeds, onions, garlic, salt, and poppy seeds. Store in an airtight container for up to 1 month.

TO PREPARE THE BREAKFAST: Arrange the tomato, avocado, and scramble on a plate. Drizzle with the oil and season with everything seasoning.

I Need Dinner
+ I Need It Now

To anyone who's ever walked into the kitchen around dinnertime only to see multiple pairs of hangry eyes, or even just their own, demanding a meal about five minutes ago: This chapter is for you. These are dishes that can be made in a jiffy but can still deliver big-time on flavor. Sheet pan dinner? Check. Simple skillet meals? I got you. One-pot quickie stir-fries? You bet. I've even thrown in a revamped version of one of the most popular recipes from my website—Chicken Parm Meatballs. Stick with me, and meltdowns will no longer be on the menu.

Shredded Chicken
Tacos with Tomatillo Salsa

When I need to get dinner into my belly stat, this is the recipe that I think of every time. It's also the poster child for meal prep: If you have this salsa ready to go and a package of boneless, skinless chicken thighs, then you can pull together an incredible dinner in almost no time. You can either go with my childhood favorite and stuff this filling into tacos, or use it to make quesadillas, enchiladas, or a burrito bowl.

Serves 3 to 4

FOR THE CHICKEN:
6 boneless skinless chicken thighs
Kosher salt and freshly cracked
   black pepper
2 tablespoons extra-virgin olive oil
1 cup (240 ml) Tomatillo Salsa
   (page 233)

FOR THE PICO DE GALLO:
1½ pounds (680 g) ripe
   tomatoes, cut into ¼ to ½-inch
   (6 to 12 mm) dice
½ large white onion, finely diced
1 to 2 jalapeño chiles, finely diced
   (for milder salsa, remove seeds and
   membranes), plus more if desired
½ cup (20 g) finely chopped fresh
   cilantro leaves
1 tablespoon fresh lime juice
Kosher salt

TO ASSEMBLE:
4 to 6 charred tortillas
1 cup (240 g) guacamole
   (see page 183)
½ cup (60 ml) crema or sour cream

TO MAKE THE CHICKEN: Season the chicken thighs with salt and pepper on both sides.

Place a large skillet over high heat and heat the oil until shimmering, about 1 minute. Using a pair of tongs, add the chicken to the skillet and sear on both sides for 3 minutes each, so that each side is golden brown.

Add the tomatillo salsa to the skillet and cover the skillet with a tight-fitting lid. Reduce the heat to medium and let the chicken cook for 20 minutes.

After 20 minutes, using a pair of tongs, flip the chicken over to the other side and continue to cook for another 10 minutes. Turn the heat off and, using 2 forks, shred the chicken and use as needed.

TO MAKE THE PICO DE GALLO: In a large bowl, combine the tomatoes, onion, jalapeños, cilantro, and lime juice. Gently toss to combine. Taste and season with salt as needed. Add extra jalapeño if you want a bit more zip.

TO ASSEMBLE THE TACOS: Place a few tablespoons of the chicken into the middle of a charred tortilla. Top with pico de gallo, guacamole, and crema. Serve immediately.

Garlic-Ginger
Crispy Chicken Stir-Fry

Everyone needs a good stir-fry recipe up their sleeve, and THIS IS IT. Seriously, it comes together in seconds, is gingery and garlicky in all the right ways, and the saucy bits are perfect for spicing up some white rice.

In a bowl whisk together the ginger, soy, vinegar, garlic, sugar, sesame oil, cornstarch, and chili paste. Stir to combine. Remove ⅓ cup (75 ml) of the marinade and set aside. Add the chicken to the remaining marinade and let sit for at least 30 minutes up to 4 hours.

Heat a large, heavy cast-iron or stainless steel skillet with a lid over high heat. Pour 1 tablespoon of the vegetable oil into the pan and swirl to coat. Use a slotted spoon to add half the chicken to the skillet, and stir and scrape the bottom with a wooden spoon. Cook chicken for about 4 minutes on each side, until golden brown. (Cover briefly, as needed, to prevent splatters.) Transfer to a plate and set aside. If your skillet has caked-on starch or burned garlic, return it to the heat and add a cupful of water to help scrape it off. Discard into the sink and wipe the skillet dry with paper towels. Heat another tablespoon of oil. Repeat with the remaining chicken.

Clean the skillet once more and pour in the remaining tablespoon of oil. Once hot, stir in the onions and sauté them until they are lightly charred but still retain some crunch, about 2 minutes. Add the chicken back in. Pour in the remaining marinade and add ⅓ cup (75 ml) water. Cook for another minute, then stir in the bok choy until wilted. Transfer to a platter and top with the crushed peanuts and basil. Serve over rice.

Serves 4-6

1 (1-inch/2.5 cm) knob fresh ginger, minced

⅓ cup (75 ml) soy sauce

2 tablespoons rice vinegar

6 cloves garlic, minced

2 tablespoons granulated sugar

2 tablespoons toasted sesame oil, plus more for drizzling

1½ tablespoons cornstarch

2 to 3 teaspoons chili paste

1½ pounds (680 g) chicken thighs, cut into 1-inch (2.5 cm) chunks (about 5 thighs)

3 tablespoons vegetable oil

1 large red onion, cut into 1-inch (2.5 cm) chunks

10 ounces (280 g) baby bok choy, roughly chopped (about 5 baby bok choy)

½ cup (75 g) dry-roasted peanuts, crushed, for garnish

½ cup (20 g) fresh Thai or traditional basil, torn

Coconut or jasmine rice, for serving

Cheesy
Hamburger Helper-Style Pasta

I was a Hamburger Helper and Rice-a-Roni kinda kid—I mean, IYKYK. Or even if you don't, this dish will make up for all the lost years when you were deprived of the ultimate meaty, creamy casserole supper. This version elevates things a bit with chives and plenty of black pepper for freshness and depth, plus chopped tomatoes instead of crushed because I love the big chunks. It's like a big hug in a bowl.

Serves 4

Extra-virgin olive oil, as needed
1 pound (455 g) lean ground beef
2 teaspoons smoked paprika
2 teaspoons dried oregano
Kosher salt and freshly ground
    black pepper
1 large yellow onion, chopped
3 cloves garlic, minced
2 tablespoons all-purpose flour
1 cup (240 ml) beef broth
1 (14½-ounce/415 g) can
    diced tomatoes
6 ounces (170 g) large pasta shells
⅔ cup (165 ml) heavy cream
1 cup (100 g) freshly grated
    Parmesan cheese, plus more
    for serving
2 cups (230 g) freshly shredded
    medium Cheddar cheese

In a 12-inch (30.5 cm) skillet over medium-high heat, warm 2 tablespoons of oil. Add the beef and cook, breaking up into small pieces, until cooked through with no pink remaining, about 8 minutes. Add 1 teaspoon of the paprika and 1 teaspoon of the oregano, then season generously with salt and pepper. Use a slotted spoon to transfer to a bowl.

Add the onion to the skillet and cook until softened, about 7 minutes. Reduce heat to medium, add the garlic, and cook for 1 more minute. Add the remaining oregano and paprika, and season with salt and pepper.

Sprinkle the flour over the onions and stir to coat, cooking until the flour gets nice and toasty, about 30 seconds. Slowly add the beef broth, stirring constantly, and bring to a boil for 30 seconds. Add the diced tomatoes and pasta shells and stir to combine.

Reduce the heat to medium-low, cover the skillet with a lid, and cook, stirring occasionally, until the pasta is al dente, 12 to 15 minutes, depending on pasta size and shape.

Uncover, increase heat to medium, then stir in the cream and the cheeses until melted and combined. Bring to a simmer and allow to reduce slightly, about 5 minutes.

Return the ground beef to the pasta and continue to cook until the beef is just heated through, about 2 minutes longer. Season with salt and pepper.

Transfer to bowls and top with more freshly grated Parmesan. Serve immediately.

Chicken Parm
Meatballs

Everyone's favorite recipe from my website felt like it needed a moment in print. These meatballs are everything you love about chicken Parm but in smaller bite-size form. They're moist, flavorful, quick to come together, and delicious whether you're tossing them with pasta or tucking them into a sub. You can stretch them all week as multi-purpose leftovers, and they even freeze well. What can I say? It's truly one of my favorite recipes of all time.

In a large bowl, combine the chicken, Parmesan, bread crumbs, egg, salt, pepper, oregano, parsley, and crushed red pepper. Carefully combine everything with your hands until the ingredients are evenly mixed.

Form the ground chicken mixture into small meatballs, each the size of a golf ball. Insert a small bocconcini ball into the center of each meatball, taking care to reform the meatball around the cheese once it's been inserted. The mozzarella should be completely hidden from sight.

Dredge each meatball in the flour to lightly coat and gently tap off any excess flour.

Preheat the oven to 350°F (175°C).

Heat the oil in a large, heavy-bottomed skillet over medium-high heat. Once the oil is hot, add half of the meatballs and sauté for 3 to 4 minutes, turning every so often to brown the outside. Once the meatballs are browned, remove them to a plate lined with a paper towel and repeat the process with the remaining meatballs. Once all meatballs are browned, drain off any excess oil, add the tomato sauce to the skillet, and place the browned meatballs on top of the sauce. Transfer the skillet, meatballs and all, into the oven and let the meatballs continue to bake for 15 to 20 minutes, until cooked through.

Remove the skillet from the oven and season with salt, pepper, and a drizzle of basil vinaigrette, and finish with fresh basil and freshly grated Parmesan if desired. Serve immediately.

Serves 4

1 pound (455 g) ground chicken
½ cup (50 g) freshly grated Parmesan cheese, plus more for serving (optional)
⅓ cup (25 g) panko bread crumbs
1 large egg
¾ teaspoon salt, plus more as needed
¾ teaspoon freshly cracked black pepper, plus more as needed
½ teaspoon dried oregano
½ teaspoon dried parsley
½ teaspoon crushed red pepper
12 to 16 bocconcini mozzarella balls
½ cup (65 g) all-purpose flour
½ cup (120 ml) extra-virgin olive oil
1 (24-ounce/680 g) jar marinara sauce
Basil Vinaigrette (page 235)
Handful of fresh basil, leaves torn, for garnish

Buffalo
Cauliflower Bowls

Welcome to the vegetarian dinner of your dreams. It's like the bar food classic got all cleaned up, with tender, crispy cauliflower shellacked in sauce and drizzled with garlicky yogurt dressing. This is a particularly great recipe if you're into meal prepping ahead of time or like to take the same thing to work for lunch all week.

Serves 4

FOR THE CAULIFLOWER:

1 large head of cauliflower, cut into medium size florets

1 tablespoon extra-virgin olive oil

1 tablespoon fresh lemon juice

½ teaspoon garlic powder

1 teaspoon kosher salt

1 teaspoon freshly cracked black pepper

½ cup (120 ml) Frank's RedHot Buffalo Wing Sauce, plus more for serving

2 tablespoons unsalted butter, melted

FOR THE BOWLS:

4 cups (790 g) cooked white rice

Zest and juice of 1 lime

2 cups (190 g) shredded purple cabbage

2 cups (480 g) black beans, rinsed and drained

1 avocado, diced or sliced

Garlic Labneh (page 234)

TO MAKE THE CAULIFLOWER: Preheat the oven to 425°F (220°C) and line a large sheet pan with parchment paper. Set aside. Transfer the cauliflower florets to a large bowl and toss with the oil, lemon juice, garlic powder, salt, and pepper.

Spread the cauliflower in a single layer over a lined sheet pan and bake for 25 to 30 minutes, gently tossing the cauliflower approximately halfway through cooking. Remove from the oven when the florets are golden brown and slightly crispy on the edges.

In a small bowl whisk together the hot sauce and melted butter. Turn the oven to broil. Pour the hot sauce mixture over the cauliflower florets and toss well to coat.

Transfer the sheet pan back into the oven and cook for an additional 2 to 3 minutes, until extra crispy. Adjust seasoning as needed.

TO ASSEMBLE THE BOWLS: Toss the white rice with the lime zest and juice, and place equal portions of the mixture into four bowls. Top each serving with about 1 cup (135 g) of the buffalo cauliflower, equal parts of the shredded cabbage, black beans, and avocado, then drizzle with the garlic labneh.

Sheet Pan Salmon with Lemon Honey Vinaigrette

I love a sheet pan recipe as much as the next girl, but so often I find that they don't actually work. The main protein is always getting undercooked while the veg goes mushy. This staple, on the other hand, gets you perfectly flaky fish, crispy yet tender veggies, and a bright lemon vinaigrette that ties it all together. If you need dinner in 20 minutes, this is IT.

TO MAKE THE VINAIGRETTE: In a small bowl, whisk together the garlic, shallot, lemon juice, honey, and olive oil.

To make the salmon: Season the salmon fillets with salt and pepper and place in a zip-top plastic bag. Add half of the marinade; reserve the other half for later. Seal the bag, removing as much air as possible, and let the salmon sit for 30 to 60 minutes.

Preheat the broiler to high with the rack set in the upper third of the oven.

On a small sheet pan, toss the asparagus with the remaining ½ tablespoon of oil, season with salt and pepper, and transfer to the oven. Broil until just starting to char, 3 to 4 minutes. Remove the salmon from the marinade and place on top of the asparagus. Spoon half of the remaining marinade over the salmon and place the pan back under the broiler until the salmon is charred around the edges, about 6 minutes.

Spoon the rest of the marinade over the top and add the scallions and Fresno pepper. Broil for 2 to 3 minutes more until the salmon is charred and medium-rare at its thickest part. Remove from the oven and let rest for a few minutes to finish any residual cooking before serving.

Serves 4

FOR THE LEMON HONEY VINAIGRETTE:
3 cloves garlic, roughly chopped

1 shallot, finely diced

2 tablespoons fresh lemon juice

1 teaspoon honey

1 tablespoon extra-virgin olive oil

FOR THE SALMON:
4 (8-ounce/225 g) skin-on center-cut salmon fillets

Kosher salt and freshly cracked black pepper

1 bunch asparagus, trimmed

4 scallions, thinly sliced

1 Fresno pepper, thinly sliced (optional)

Shrimp Fried Rice

It would be impossible to write a book dedicated to simple, easy meals and not include fried rice. It's pretty much as straightforward, no-nonsense, and versatile as it gets—like the Swiss Army knife of dinner. You'll notice that I call for using day-old rice. That's because rice that's lost a little bit of its moisture will get nice and crispy for you. But don't sweat it if you don't have that prepped, you can also make a batch of rice, place it in a flat layer on a sheet pan, and pop it into the freezer for about an hour! Boom—you're in business.

Serves 4

5 tablespoons canola oil, plus more as needed
1 pound (455 g) medium shrimp, peeled and deveined, with tails intact
Kosher salt
1 yellow onion, diced
3 cloves garlic, minced
1 heaping cup (60 g) sugar snap peas, halved on the bias
3 cups (615 g) day-old cooked white rice (see headnote)
3 large eggs, beaten
3 teaspoons soy sauce
16 fresh basil leaves, cut chiffonade

In a wok over high heat, warm 3 tablespoons of the oil. Season shrimp lightly with salt, add to the wok, and cook until opaque, about 3 minutes. Transfer the shrimp to a plate.

Warm the remaining 2 tablespoons oil in the wok. Add the onion and cook until softened, about 5 minutes. Add the garlic and cook for 1 more minute.

Add the rice and cook, stirring occasionally, until heated through and starting to soften, about 2 minutes. Add more oil as needed if the rice begins to stick to the wok.

Add the soy sauce and sugar snap peas and stir to combine.

Push the rice to one side of the wok and add the eggs. Stir constantly with a wooden spoon to softly scramble, then mix in with rice.

Return the shrimp to the wok, toss to coat, and cook until heated through, about 1 minute.

Season with salt, then fold half of the basil into the rice. Garnish with the remaining basil and serve immediately.

Sausage
Sheet Pan Supper

I know that a recipe is legit when I end up eating it multiple days in a row.
Considering I'm always cooking and stocking my fridge with leftovers, that's high
praise! Well, this dish definitely makes that list of distinction because I put these
sausages to work for four days straight after the first time I made them.
I love the way the cherry tomatoes freshen everything up while balancing out
the pepper and onion moment. Oh, and don't skimp on the Calabrian vin as
a condiment—you won't regret it.

Preheat the oven to 400°F (205°C).

In a bowl, combine the yellow, red, and orange bell peppers with the onions
and tomatoes. Drizzle with oil and season with kosher salt. Spread into an even
layer on a sheet pan.

Roast in the oven for 20 minutes, until the vegetables have softened and
started to char.

Remove the pan and arrange the sausages on top, then return to the oven
and roast until the vegetables are very tender and the sausages are browned,
15 to 20 minutes longer. Serve with Calabrian vinaigrette, if desired.

Serves 4 to 6

1 yellow bell pepper,
    seeded and sliced
1 red bell pepper,
    seeded and sliced
1 orange bell pepper,
    seeded and sliced
1 yellow onion, thinly sliced
1 pint (290 g) cherry tomatoes
¼ cup (60 ml) extra-virgin olive oil
Kosher salt
6 mild or spicy Italian sausages
Calabrian Vinaigrette
    (page 231, optional)

Salads + Other Things to Eat in Bowls

Bright, fresh salads and other things to eat in bowls have been What's Gaby Cooking mainstays from the early days—namely because they're what I'm reaching for most of the time in my own kitchen. Especially during the week, when I need meals to come together ASAP, these are the recipes that save my butt every time. And let me tell you, this new batch of dishes is next level.

BBQ Chicken
Chopped Salad

Damn, I love this salad. I have a special place in my heart for any salad with
a mayo- or sour cream–based dressing, but the herby buttermilk dressing I whipped
up for this takes creamy dressings to an even fresher, tangier place. Otherwise,
I stayed pretty true to the original CPK classic. Don't fix what's not broke, ya know?

Serves 4 to 6

FOR THE TORTILLA STRIPS:
⅔ cup (165 ml) canola oil, for frying
6 small corn tortillas, cut into
 ¼-inch (6 mm) strips
Kosher salt

FOR THE SALAD:
1 head iceberg lettuce, chopped
6 ounces (170 g) jicama, diced
2 tablespoons finely chopped
 fresh cilantro
1 tablespoon finely chopped
 fresh basil
1 cup (145 g) corn (canned and
 drained or fresh)
1 (15-ounce/430 g) can black beans,
 drained
1 cup (115 g) shredded Monterey
 Jack cheese
1 recipe Herby Buttermilk Ranch
 (page 230)
3 cups (585 g) shredded chicken
1 cup (240 ml) of your favorite
 barbecue sauce, plus more
 for serving, if desired
Kosher salt
1 pint (290 g) cherry tomatoes,
 halved
1 avocado, sliced
4 scallions, sliced

TO MAKE THE TORTILLA STRIPS: In a large Dutch oven or high-walled
skillet, pour canola oil 1-inch (2.5 cm) deep and heat to 350°F (175°C) on
a deep-fry thermometer.

In batches, add the tortilla strips and cook for 30 seconds. Use a spider
or tongs to flip the tortilla strips and cook for an additional 30 seconds on
the other side, until golden. Transfer to a plate lined with a paper towel and
sprinkle with salt. Set aside.

TO ASSEMBLE THE SALAD: In a large bowl, combine the iceberg,
jicama, cilantro, basil, corn, beans, and cheese. Toss with three-quarters of
the dressing. Transfer to serving bowls.

In a medium bowl, combine the shredded chicken with the barbecue sauce
and a pinch of salt. Top the salads with the barbecue chicken, tomatoes,
avocado, scallions, and tortilla strips. Drizzle with more dressing and barbecue
sauce, if desired.

Chopped Salad
Chorizo

Does it get any more fun than a chopped salad? This version has the same every-thing-but-the-kitchen-sink appeal with spiced pepitas, tons of veggies, and avocado (duh), plus a sweet-tart honey-lime vinaigrette to cut the richness of the chorizo-cotija combo. I can honestly say this is one of my favorite ginormous salads to date, and what makes it even better is how well it holds up when prepped in advance.

TO MAKE THE SPICED PEPITAS: Place the pepitas in a dry medium-size skillet over medium heat. Cook, stirring frequently, until nice and toasty, about 4 minutes. Add the olive oil and stir to coat, then add the cumin and paprika and sprinkle with salt. Remove from the heat and allow to cool.

TO PREPARE THE CHORIZO: Heat the canola oil in a medium skillet over medium-high heat. Add the chorizo and lightly sauté until a little golden brown.

TO ASSEMBLE THE SALAD: In a large bowl, combine the romaine, kale, chopped cilantro, red bell pepper, onion, radishes, tomatoes, corn, half the cotija, and half the avocado and toss with the dressing. Transfer to serving bowls and top with the chorizo, spiced pepitas, the remaining cotija and avocado, and cilantro leaves.

Serves 4

FOR THE SPICED PEPITAS:
½ cup (65 grams) pepitas
1 tablespoon extra-virgin olive oil
1 teaspoon ground cumin
1 teaspoon smoked paprika
Kosher salt

FOR THE CHORIZO:
1 tablespoon canola oil
12 ounces (340 g) cured chorizo, casings peeled off, chopped into ½-inch (12 mm) pieces

FOR THE SALAD:
1 head romaine, finely chopped
1 bunch dinosaur kale, finely chopped
½ cup (20 g) finely chopped fresh cilantro, plus whole leaves for garnish
1 red bell pepper, cut into small dice
1 small red onion, cut into small dice
5 radishes, thinly sliced on a mandolin
2 Roma tomatoes, cut into small dice
1 cup (145 g) corn (fresh, canned and drained, or frozen and thawed)
4 ounces (115 g) cotija, crumbled
1 large or 2 small avocados, diced
Honey Lime Vinaigrette (page 230)

Steak Salad with Focaccia Croutons

I feel zero shame when I tell you that I once ate this salad for three days straight. It's just that good. It hits all the right hearty, meaty notes for lunch and dinner, and it gets a bright facelift from a zingy Calabrian chile vinaigrette. There's no need to make the focaccia from scratch because store-bought works perfectly here, but you could repurpose any leftover Cacio e Pepe Focaccia (page 103) that you may have.

Serves 4

FOR THE STEAK:

1 pound (455 g) hanger or skirt steak, resting at room temperature for 30 minutes

½ teaspoon kosher salt

½ teaspoon freshly ground black pepper

3 teaspoons ground Aleppo pepper (or 2½ teaspoons paprika and ½ teaspoon cayenne pepper)

2 tablespoons canola oil

FOR THE FOCACCIA CROUTONS:

8 ounces (225 g) day-old focaccia, torn into 1-inch (2.5 cm) pieces

Extra-virgin olive oil, for drizzling

Kosher salt

FOR THE SALAD:

6 cups (120 g) loosely packed arugula

Pinch kosher salt

3 Persian cucumbers, thinly sliced

2 large heirloom tomatoes, sliced into wedges

1 red onion, thinly sliced

Calabrian Vinaigrette (page 231)

1 ounce (28 g) freshly shaved Parmesan cheese

Flaky salt, for serving

TO MAKE THE STEAKS: Preheat a cast-iron skillet over high heat. Rub the hanger with the salt, black pepper, and Aleppo pepper. Add the canola oil to the skillet and allow to heat for 30 to 45 seconds, until just beginning to smoke. Add the steak and cook to desired doneness, turning once, 4 to 5 minutes per side. Transfer to a cutting board and allow to rest for 10 minutes, then slice against the grain.

TO MAKE THE CROUTONS: Wipe the cast-iron skillet dry with paper towels and preheat over medium-high heat. Liberally drizzle the focaccia pieces with olive oil so there are no dry spots and season with salt. Cook in the skillet, stirring occasionally, until golden and toasted, about 5 minutes. If necessary, do this in two batches so as to not overcrowd the skillet.

TO ASSEMBLE THE SALAD: In a large bowl, toss the arugula with a pinch of kosher salt. Add the cucumbers, tomatoes, and red onion and toss with half of the dressing. Top with the steak, croutons, and shaved Parmesan. Drizzle with the remaining dressing and season with flaky salt before serving.

Crab Cake Salad

You can never go wrong with such a tried-and-true seafood classic, but I obviously had to jazz it up just a little, which included transforming the whole dish into a salad that manages to feel filling enough for a meal but exciting enough for an appetizer. Fried capers add some salty kick while crisp butter or Boston lettuce keeps things light and fresh. (Though you could use romaine instead.)

TO MAKE THE CRAB CAKES: In a bowl, whisk together the mayonnaise, egg, mustards, Worcestershire, and 1 tablespoon of the capers until smooth. In another bowl, toss the crabmeat with the panko. Fold in the mayonnaise mixture. Then season with a pinch of kosher salt and a few generous grinds of black pepper. Do not overmix. Cover and chill for 1 hour or up to overnight.

Line a sheet pan or large plate with parchment paper. Scoop out 8 equal portions of the crab cake mixture (about ⅓ cup/45 g each) and lightly pack into a patty. (The key here is to lightly pack them so you get tender crab cakes.)

In a large skillet over medium-high heat, heat 2 tablespoons of the canola oil. Add the remaining 3 tablespoons of drained capers and cook until they pop open and begin to brown and crisp, stirring occasionally, about 3 minutes. Transfer the fried capers to a paper towel–lined plate and set aside.

Pour the remaining ¼ cup (60 ml) canola oil to the skillet and warm until shimmering. Add the crab cakes, being sure not to overcrowd the pan, and cook until deeply golden brown, 3 to 4 minutes per side.

Transfer to a plate and sprinkle lightly with salt. Cover with foil to keep warm while you prepare the salad.

TO ASSEMBLE THE SALAD: In a large bowl, toss the lettuce lightly with the vinaigrette. Transfer to plates or a large serving platter. Top with the avocado, chives, and warm crab cakes. Top the crab cakes with a generous dollop of tartar sauce, a few generous grinds of black pepper, and the fried capers before serving.

Serves 4 for a dinner salad
or 8 for an appetizer

FOR THE CRAB CAKES:
½ cup (120 ml) mayonnaise
1 large egg
2 heaping teaspoons Dijon mustard
2 heaping teaspoons whole grain mustard
1 tablespoon Worcestershire sauce
4 tablespoons drained capers
1 pound (455 g) fresh jumbo lump crabmeat
⅔ cup (80 g) panko or crushed saltine crackers
Kosher salt and freshly ground black pepper
2 tablespoons plus ¼ cup (60 ml) canola oil

FOR THE SALAD:
14 ounces (400 g) butter lettuce leaves, little gems, or heart of romaine
Honey Dijon Vinaigrette (page 231)
2 avocados, cubed
1 small bunch chives, minced
Tartar sauce, for serving
Freshly ground black pepper

Crispy Rice
+ Blackened Chicken Salad

Blackened chicken, along with blackened salmon, are my protein love languages, and both are amazing alongside this perfectly crispy rice. The whole lot gets smothered in Miso Sesame Vinaigrette (page 231), a dressing so good I've honestly considered whether it's acceptable to bathe in it.

Serves 4

FOR THE BLACKENED CHICKEN:

6 tablespoons plus 2 tablespoons unsalted butter

2 teaspoons ground cumin

2 teaspoons granulated garlic

2 teaspoons smoked paprika

2 teaspoons sweet paprika

2½ teaspoons kosher salt

2 boneless skinless chicken breasts

1 lime, cut in half

FOR THE CRISPY RICE:

¼ cup (60 ml) canola oil

2 cups (400 g) cooled cooked rice

Kosher salt

FOR THE SALAD:

2 heaping packed cups (190 g) shredded red cabbage (about ½ large head)

2 heaping packed cups (190 g) shredded green cabbage (about ½ large head)

2 large carrots, peeled and ribboned

¾ cup (30 g) roughly chopped fresh cilantro

1 bunch scallions, trimmed and sliced

Miso Sesame Vinaigrette (page 231)

½ cup (55 g) toasted peanuts

1 tablespoon white or black sesame seeds

Lime wedges, for serving (see Note)

TO MAKE THE BLACKENED CHICKEN: In a large microwave-safe bowl, melt 6 tablespoons of the butter. Stir in the cumin, granulated garlic, both paprikas, and salt. Dry the chicken breasts well with paper towels. Add the chicken to the bowl and turn to coat in the butter mixture. Allow to sit for 20 to 30 minutes at room temperature.

In a large cast-iron skillet over medium-high heat, melt the remaining 2 tablespoons butter, tilting the skillet to coat. Add the chicken and cook until it is thoroughly charred on one side, about 7 minutes. Flip and continue to cook until the internal temperature reaches 165°F (74°C) on an instant-read thermometer, 6 to 8 minutes longer. Transfer to a cutting board and squeeze with lime. Wipe the skillet dry with paper towels.

TO MAKE THE CRISPY RICE: Return the skillet to the stovetop over medium-high heat and pour in the oil. Once the oil is shimmering, add the rice and sprinkle with salt. Using a spatula, press the rice into a tight even layer and cook until the underside is crispy and golden, 5 to 7 minutes. Flip and continue to cook until totally crispy, breaking up with a spatula as you go.

TO ASSEMBLE THE SALAD: In a large bowl, combine the red and green cabbage, carrots, cilantro, scallions, and crispy rice. Toss with almost all the dressing, then top with sliced blackened chicken, peanuts, and sesame seeds. Spoon the remaining dressing over the chicken. Serve with lime wedges.

NOTE: Alternatively, garnish with fresh mint, chopped scallions, or other fresh herbs.

Teriyaki
Chicken Salad

Somehow, between the hundreds of recipes I've developed for my website and previous three cookbooks, I've never done a teriyaki recipe until now. What is wrong with this picture? I'm finally righting this major wrong with the perfect weeknight meal that puts everything you could possibly want in a bowl and slathers it in sticky, sweet, salty goodness.

TO MAKE THE CHICKEN: In a medium bowl, whisk together 1¼ cup (300 ml) water with the soy, sugar, honey, garlic, sesame oil, ginger, and pepper. Reserve ½ cup (120 ml) of the sauce in a container and refrigerate until needed. Add the cornstarch to the remaining sauce and whisk again. Put the chicken in a shallow 8 by 8-inch (20 by 20 cm) baking dish and pour the sauce over the top. Flip the chicken over to evenly coat with the sauce and place skin side up, uncovered, in the fridge for at least 1 hour or up to 8 hours. Bring to room temperature 20 minutes before grilling.

FOR THE GRILL: Preheat a grill pan or outdoor grill to medium-high on one side and medium-low on the other. Grill your chicken skin side down until golden and charred, 3 to 4 minutes. (Remember, you have honey and sugar in the marinade so, if needed, move the chicken to the cooler side of the grill to prevent overly charred results.) Flip the thighs over, and if using an outdoor grill, cover with the lid and cook for another 5 minutes. If using a grill pan, cook and cover with a large bowl. Cook both sides until juices run clear when pierced with a paring knife. Transfer to a plate to rest.

Brush the broccoli with some of the remaining sauce and grill until nicely marked and bright green, about 2 minutes on each side. Thread 4 skewers with 6 tomatoes each, then brush with some sauce and grill until the skins are split and slightly charred all over, about 4 minutes. Thread 4 more skewers with 3 onion wedges each, then brush with sauce and grill until nicely charred, about 3 minutes per side.

TO ASSEMBLE THE SALAD: Toss the cabbage and cilantro in a large bowl with the dressing and divide evenly among four wide bowls. Place one piece of chicken in each (you can slice or leave whole) then divide the broccoli evenly among the bowls. Remove one skewer's worth of tomatoes and one of onions into each bowl. And finally, divide the mango and lime wedges among the bowls and enjoy.

Serves 4

FOR THE CHICKEN:
- ⅓ cup (75 ml) soy sauce
- ¼ cup (50 g) granulated sugar
- 1 tablespoon honey
- 1 teaspoon granulated garlic
- 1 teaspoon sesame oil
- ½ teaspoon ground ginger
- ½ teaspoon freshly ground black pepper
- 1½ tablespoons cornstarch
- 4 large chicken thighs, boneless with skin

FOR THE SALAD:
- 8 ounces (225 g) broccoli, cut into large spears
- 1 cup (145 g) cherry tomatoes
- 1 medium red onion, cut into thin wedges with root end intact
- 2 pounds (910 g) Napa cabbage (about three-fourths of a large head), thinly sliced
- ½ cup (20 g) roughly chopped fresh cilantro
- 1 recipe Teriyaki Lime Dressing (page 233)
- 1 mango, diced
- Lime wedges, for serving

Green Tahini
Little Gem + Beet Salad

I know that I have a tendency to want to swim in a lot of the dressings and sauces I create, but this green tahini, with all of its fresh dill and a tangy pop of pomegranate molasses, truly takes the cake. The next best thing is drizzling it all over this substantial beet-filled salad that doesn't want for anything but would be perfectly at home with the Perfect Steak (page 115).

Serves 4 to 6

FOR THE GREEN TAHINI DRESSING
(makes about ⅔ cup/165 ml):

¼ cup (8 g) chopped fresh dill fronds and stems, plus more fronds for garnishing

⅓ cup (75 ml) tahini paste

1 tablespoon pomegranate molasses

1 tablespoon honey

2½ teaspoons sea salt

⅓ cup (75 ml) extra-virgin olive oil

FOR THE SALAD:

2 bunches baby yellow beets, washed and trimmed

2 bunches baby red beets, washed and trimmed

2 tablespoons extra-virgin olive oil

Kosher salt

4 gem lettuce heads, cored, separated, and washed

1 Hass avocado, cut into chunks

½ cup (40 g) store-bought roasted chickpeas in sea salt, crushed

TO MAKE THE DRESSING: In a blender, pulse the dill, ⅓ cup (75 ml) water, tahini, pomegranate molasses, honey, and salt to combine. With the blender running at the lowest speed, drizzle the oil through the opening in the lid until a creamy dressing forms. Transfer to a bowl and set aside. Extra dressing will keep for two weeks tightly sealed in the refrigerator.

TO PREPARE THE SALAD: Preheat the oven to 350°F (175°C). Tear off two large foil sheets to create foil pouches and place the yellow beets in one and the red in the other. Drizzle 1 tablespoon of the oil over each and season with salt. Toss to coat. Fold the foil precisely to keep the beets and steam from escaping, crimping the edges to seal tightly. Set the two pouches on a sheet pan and bake for 45 minutes. Remove from the oven and carefully uncrimp the foil to release the steam before opening fully. Insert a paring knife into the largest beets to check for tenderness. The knife should meet no resistance, and the beets' skin should slide right off. If not, reseal the pouches and bake for another 10 to 15 minutes until tender. Let cool in the bags for 15 minutes, then remove and slip the beet skins off using paper towels. Slice into halves or quarters depending on size and set aside.

TO ASSEMBLE THE SALAD: In a large bowl, toss the lettuce with about 3 tablespoons of the dressing and a couple pinches of salt to coat the leaves evenly. Transfer to a serving platter. Repeat this with the yellow beets, then the red, and arrange them over the greens—this prevents the beets from bleeding their color all over the lettuce. Top with the slices of avocado, roasted chickpeas, and fresh dill fronds. Drizzle with extra dressing and serve.

Sesame-Ginger Chicken + Rice Bowl

I ate this salad on repeat the entire time I was pregnant with Poppy
(at least, once I got my appetite back after the first trimester), and it continues
to be one of my all-time favorites.

TO MAKE THE DRESSING: Add the soy, vinegar, and honey to a medium bowl. Combine the avocado oil and sesame oil in a spouted cup, then slowly drizzle it into the bowl while whisking constantly. Set aside.

TO MAKE THE SALAD: In a shallow glass baking dish, combine the soy sauce, sesame oil, vinegar, ginger, garlic, and 1 teaspoon black pepper. Add the chicken and toss to evenly coat. Cover with plastic wrap and refrigerate for 2 to 4 hours.

In a medium saucepan with a lid, combine the rice (do not rinse), water, and 1½ teaspoons sea salt with the star anise and cinnamon stick (if using). Stir together and bring to a boil over medium-high heat. Reduce to a simmer, cover, and cook until the water is absorbed and the rice is tender, 30 to 40 minutes. Check for doneness and either cook a few more minutes or remove from the heat and let sit covered for 10 minutes before fluffing with a fork.

While the rice is cooking, preheat a broiler to high and position a rack 6 inches (15 cm) from the top. Cover a sheet pan with foil and set a wire rack on top. Remove the chicken from the marinade and place on the rack. Broil until charred and cooked through, about 4 minutes on each side. Let rest until cool enough to handle and then slice into thin strips.

Divide the bok choy among four shallow bowls, then add the rice, chicken, carrots, and bell pepper. Drizzle some dressing over the top. In another bowl, mix the cilantro, basil, and mint, then divide among the salad servings, placing the herbs in the center of each. Garnish the salads with almonds, coconut flakes, and lime wedges, if using, and serve.

Serves 4

FOR THE DRESSING:
3 tablespoons soy sauce
2 tablespoons rice wine vinegar
1 tablespoon honey
¼ cup (60 ml) avocado, peanut, or favorite oil
3 tablespoons sesame oil

FOR THE SALAD:
¼ cup (60 ml) soy sauce
2 tablespoons sesame oil
2 tablespoons rice wine vinegar
1 tablespoon freshly grated ginger
4 cloves garlic
Sea salt and freshly ground black pepper
5 boneless, skinless chicken thighs
1½ cups (300 g) black rice
2¾ cups (660 ml) cold water
1 star anise pod or ½ teaspoon ground anise (optional)
1 cinnamon stick (optional)
12 ounces (340 g) baby bok choy, thinly sliced
1½ heaping cups (4 ounces/115 g) shredded carrots
1 yellow bell pepper, thinly sliced
½ cup (20 g) roughly chopped fresh cilantro leaves and stems
⅓ cup (10 g) fresh Thai basil leaves, torn
⅓ cup (10 g) fresh mint leaves, torn
¼ cup (25 g) toasted sliced almonds (optional)
¼ cup (20 g) toasted coconut flakes (optional)
Lime wedges (optional)

Peak Summer Vibes Dinner Party

Full menu serves 6 to 8

My favorite time to entertain, hands down, is the summer. Recipes bursting with fresh produce; rosé on repeat; the warm, balmy nights that make everyone want to sit around chatting until ten p.m.—it's heaven. This menu is dedicated to that perfect entertaining season, when all you want to do is cook something effortless and light. These dishes will make it feel like you've popped by the local farm and just given everything a little zhuzh to pull together an expertly polished meal. It includes another one of my favorite salmon recipes, in addition to the slow-roasted version in "The Ultimates" (page 92), because I say the more salmon, the better. Just add a round of Thomas's specialty Aperol Tequila Spritzes and plenty of good company.

Aperol Tequila Spritz

2 cups (480 ml) tequila
1 cup (240 ml) fresh lime juice (about 16 limes)
1 cup (240 ml) Aperol
8 to 10 dashes orange bitters
Topo Chico, to top

In a large pitcher, stir together the tequila, lime juice, Aperol, and bitters until combined.

When ready to serve, pour over ice and top each glass with a few ounces of Topo Chico or your favorite sparkling water. Serve immediately.

Marinated Burrata with Crostini

⅓ cup (75 ml) extra-virgin olive oil
3 cloves garlic, finely chopped
Pinch crushed red pepper
1 to 2 (8-ounce/225 g) balls Burrata cheese
Fresh basil, for garnish
Ciabatta crostini

In a small nonstick skillet, heat the oil over low heat. Add the garlic and crushed red pepper flakes and sauté for 45 seconds. Remove from the heat and let cool entirely.

Transfer the whole ball(s) of Burrata onto a small serving platter. Once the oil has cooled, drizzle it on top of the cheese. Top with basil and serve with crostini.

Baby Romaine with a Side of Croutons + Parmesan

6 to 8 heads baby romaine lettuce
Lemon Shallot Vinaigrette
  (page 235)
1 cup (100 g) finely grated fresh Parmesan cheese
2 cups (90 g) homemade croutons (see page 66)

Carefully trim the lettuce leaves off the head, keeping them intact. Rinse well and dry.

In a large salad bowl, toss the lettuce leaves with the lemon shallot vinaigrette and grate the fresh Parm on top. Add the croutons and serve.

Pasta with Burst Sun Golds
Summer

In a large skillet, combine the tomatoes and oil over medium-high heat.

As the oil starts to get hot and the tomatoes start to blister, reduce the heat to medium and let simmer for 20 minutes, stirring occasionally. In the last 5 minutes, add the garlic, salt, black pepper, and crushed red pepper and stir to combine.

Once the tomatoes start to fall apart, remove them from the heat and let cool in the skillet for about 20 minutes. Stir in the basil to wilt and add the corn. Adjust salt and black pepper as needed.

Cook the pasta until al dente while the tomatoes are cooling. Drain the pasta and add to the tomato and corn mixture. Adjust the seasoning as needed and serve with fresh basil.

2 pounds (910 g) Sun Gold tomatoes, quartered

½ cup (120 ml) extra-virgin olive oil

6 cloves garlic, finely chopped

Kosher salt and freshly cracked black pepper

1 teaspoon crushed red pepper

½ bunch fresh basil, plus more for serving

3 ears corn on the cob, kernels sliced to remove

1½ pounds (680 g) mafaldine pasta

Easy Side of Salmon with Tomatoes + Basil

FOR THE SALMON:

1 (2-pound/910 g) side of salmon, pin bones removed

⅓ cup (75 ml) extra-virgin olive oil

4 cloves garlic, minced

Kosher salt and freshly cracked black pepper

2 teaspoons ground cumin

2 teaspoons paprika

½ teaspoon dried oregano

½ teaspoon crushed red pepper

FOR THE TOPPING:

1 pint (290 g) cherry tomatoes, halved

½ cup (120 ml) Basil Vinaigrette (page 235)

Kosher salt and freshly cracked black pepper

To make the salmon: Place the large piece of fish on a parchment-lined sheet pan and preheat the oven to 425°F (220°C).

Combine the oil, garlic, salt, black pepper, cumin, paprika, oregano, and crushed red pepper into a loose paste. Brush all over the fish.

Transfer the fish to the sheet pan and bake in the preheated oven until done, 8 to 10 minutes. For the last minute, turn the oven to broil to crisp the top.

Remove the fish from the oven and let rest for 5 minutes.

To make the topping: Combine the halved cherry tomatoes with the basil vinaigrette and season with salt and black pepper.

Transfer large pieces of the salmon onto a serving platter. Toss the cherry tomato basil mixture on top and serve.

Peach + Raspberry Cobbler

TO MAKE THE COBBLER TOPPING: Preheat the oven to 375°F (190°C). In a large bowl, whisk together the flour, granulated sugar, baking powder, cinnamon, and salt. Add the butter. Using your fingertips, incorporate until only small lumps of butter remain. Gently stir in sour cream and heavy cream and knead until a biscuit-like dough forms. If it's too thick, add a few more teaspoons of heavy cream to bring the dough together.

TO MAKE THE FRUIT FILLING: In a large bowl, combine the peaches, raspberries, flour, brown sugar, juice, zest, and salt. Transfer to a medium-size skillet or baking dish, 9 to 10 inches (23 to 25 cm) in diameter.

TO ASSEMBLE: Tear the biscuit dough into pieces, or scoop into balls, and scatter over the fruit, leaving some of the fruit exposed. Transfer the cobbler into the oven and bake until the juices are thick and bubbling and the topping is cooked through and golden brown, 45 to 50 minutes. Let cool for at least 1 hour. Scoop ice cream on top and serve.

FOR THE COBBLER TOPPING:

- 1½ cups (185 g) all-purpose flour
- 3 tablespoons granulated sugar
- 1½ teaspoons baking powder
- ¾ teaspoon ground cinnamon
- ½ teaspoon kosher salt
- 6 tablespoons unsalted butter, chilled and grated
- ½ cup (120 ml) plus 1 tablespoon sour cream
- ¼ to ½ cup (60 to 120 ml) heavy cream
- Vanilla ice cream, for serving

FOR THE FRUIT FILLING:

- 8 ripe peaches
- 1½ cups (85 g) raspberries
- 1 tablespoon all-purpose flour
- 2 tablespoons brown sugar
- 1 teaspoon fresh lemon juice
- 1 teaspoon freshly grated lemon zest
- 1 teaspoon kosher salt

The Ultimates

This chapter is dedicated to the go-tos. The hits-the-spot-every-timers. The gotta-have-'ems. You've got your Bolognese, your fried chicken, and your seafood boil pasta. We're playing all the hits so you can indulge in these tried-and-trues anytime the mood strikes. You're gonna want to bookmark these dishes for dinner parties and special occasions because they're a surefire way to impress. But don't let weekdays feel left out; these recipes are just as suitable (and manageable) for everyday dinners too.

Fried Baja Fish Tacos with Pickled Slaw

I live for a fish taco. Ever since our south-of-the-border adventures in high school, this classic meal has had my heart. I'm pleased to report that I've nailed the best possible approximation of those perfect crispy fried fish tacos and pickled slaw.

Serves 4 to 6

FOR THE PICKLED SLAW:

½ teaspoon cumin seeds

1 cinnamon stick

1 cup (240 ml) apple cider vinegar

2 tablespoons granulated sugar

1 teaspoon kosher salt

2 cloves garlic, smashed

¾ cup (85 g) thinly sliced red onion

3 cups(280 g) thinly sliced
   green cabbage

1 cup (110 g) carrots, shredded

FOR THE FISH:

6 cups (1.4 L) frying oil

1¼ cups (155 g) all-purpose flour

½ cup (65 g) cornstarch,
   plus more for dredging

1 teaspoon baking powder

1 teaspoon kosher salt

¾ teaspoon ground cumin

½ teaspoon chipotle powder

½ teaspoon baking soda

1¾ cup (420 ml) sparkling water

2 tablespoons vodka

1½ pounds cod or hake fish,
   cut into 1-inch-thick (2.5 cm),
   3 to 4-inch (7.5 to 10 cm)
   long strips (4 to 5 pieces)

FOR THE TOPPINGS:

¼ to ½ cup (60 to 120 ml) sour cream

12 corn tortillas

Fresh cilantro sprigs, for garnish

1 serrano chile, thinly sliced

1 lime, cut into wedges

TO MAKE THE SLAW: In a medium saucepan, toast the cumin seeds and cinnamon stick until fragrant. Add the vinegar, 1 cup (240 ml) water, the sugar, salt, and garlic. Bring to a boil, then reduce to a simmer for 8 minutes. Add the onions and let cool until just warm. Put the cabbage and carrots in a bowl, then pour the onions over the top and toss together. Let sit for 15 minutes.

TO MAKE THE FISH: Preheat the oil in a 3½ quart (3.3 L) Dutch oven or cast-iron pot to 375°F (190°C).

In a large bowl, whisk together the flour, cornstarch, baking powder, salt, cumin, chipotle powder, and baking soda. Stir in the sparkling water and vodka, then set aside.

Pat the fish dry with paper towels and dust them with cornstarch until lightly covered all over.

Dip the fish pieces into the batter and then carefully lay them into the oil. Fry until lightly golden and crispy, about 5 minutes. Transfer to a sheet pan lined with a paper towel.

TO SERVE: Put the sour cream in a small bowl and stir in 1 tablespoon or more of the slaw liquid to make a nice drizzling sauce. Warm the tortillas on the stovetop or in a microwave. Put a few chunks of fish on each tortilla then top with some slaw, cilantro sprigs, sour cream, and a few serrano slices. Serve with lime wedges on the side.

Korean BBQ–Inspired Meatloaf

I don't know how, but I've made it twelve-plus years in the recipe game and have yet to make a meatloaf. Well, that ends now. I've finally taken on the old-school classic and have given it a modern Korean twist with kimchi, Korean chili powder, and gochujang (fermented red chili paste). Slice it up and serve it over rice, or roll the mixture into meatballs and cook it that way, if it's more your vibe.

Adjust an oven rack in the middle of the oven and preheat to 375°F (190°C). Spray a 9 by 5-inch (23 by 12 cm) loaf pan with nonstick cooking spray and set aside.

TO MAKE THE MEATLOAF: In a large bowl, combine the beef, bacon, rice, kimchi, carrots, chopped white and light green parts of the scallions, the celery, sesame oil, salt, chili powder, garlic powder, and egg. Using gloved hands, mix everything together until evenly combined. Form into a loaf about the same size as the pan, then transfer and press into the prepared pan. With the short side of the pan facing you, make a ½-inch (12 mm) space with your hands on each long side of the meatloaf. This will allow space for the drippings.

Bake for 25 to 30 minutes until the internal temperature reaches 110°F (43°C). Top with the gochujang sauce and return to the oven and bake until the sauce is set, another 10 minutes.

TO SERVE: Let the meatloaf rest in the pan for 20 minutes before serving. Slice and lay over a bed of rice tossed with the dark green scallion slices, and top with the toasted nori and sesame seeds.

Serves 4 to 6

FOR THE MEATLOAF:

1½ pounds (680 g) 80 percent lean ground beef

6 slices bacon, minced

¾ cup (97 g) cooked rice, such as jasmine

¼ cup (36 g) kimchi, roughly chopped

½ cup (70 g) shredded and chopped carrots

8 scallions, white and light green parts chopped and dark green parts separated and thinly sliced

½ cup (50 g) finely chopped celery

1 tablespoon sesame oil

1½ teaspoons kosher salt

1 to 2 teaspoons Korean chili powder

½ teaspoon garlic powder

1 large egg

¼ cup (60 ml) gochujang, plus more for serving

FOR SERVING:

Cooked rice

Nori strips or sheets, toasted, for garnish

Sesame seeds, toasted, for garnish

Modern-Day
Pasta Salad

Let's be honest, pasta salads tend to be boring AF. Or they're all gooped up with mayo (no offense to mayo—I love you, just not in a pasta salad). Well, this is not that. We've gone full-on Mediterranean because that's where my mind is these days, and what pasta dish doesn't get better with a dose of sunshine from sun-dried tomatoes, arugula, and an herby shallot vinaigrette?

Serves 6 to 8

1 pound (455 g) rotini pasta, cooked and drained

8 ounces (225 g) ciliegine (cherry-size) mozzarella balls, drained

1 pint (290 g) cherry tomatoes, halved

⅓ cup (35 g) packed sun-dried tomatoes, roughly chopped, plus oil from the jar

6 ounces (170 g) salami, cubed

1 cup (20 g) tightly packed arugula

1 recipe Herby Shallot Vinaigrette (page 232)

Kosher salt and freshly cracked black pepper

Crushed red pepper

Flaky salt, for serving

In a large bowl, toss the pasta with the mozzarella balls, cherry tomatoes, sun-dried tomatoes, salami, and arugula. Combine with the vinaigrette.

Season with kosher salt and black pepper, as needed, and crushed red pepper, as desired. Transfer to a serving bowl and drizzle lightly with oil from the sun dried tomatoes. Allow to sit for at least 1 hour or up to overnight, then top with more freshly cracked black pepper, crushed red pepper, and flaky salt before serving.

Cacio e Pepe Focaccia

Focaccia can be a little bit prissy and a lotta-bit fussy, but it's also one of the ultimate breads that tops my list every time—soft, chewy, and salty. Delish. So, I simplified things by making this a one-bowl recipe (versus needing a stand mixer) and no-knead too. You still have to let the dough rise twice, but you can set a timer and be done. Enjoy this hot out of the pan with a healthy drizzle of EVOO.

In a medium bowl, whisk together the yeast and the sugar. Add the warm water and whisk to combine. Cover with a kitchen towel and allow the yeast to bloom for 5 minutes. The mixture should look bubbly and alive. If not, start over. Meanwhile, in another bowl, whisk together the flour and kosher salt. Add the flour mixture to the yeast mixture and stir until a wet dough forms and you can't see any more flour. Do not overmix.

Coat a large bowl with 5 tablespoons (75 ml) of the oil. Carefully transfer the dough into the bowl and turn to coat in the oil. Cover with a greased piece of plastic wrap and refrigerate to ferment, at least 8 hours or up to 24. The dough should double in size.

Remove from the fridge and allow to sit out for 20 minutes. Use an additional 4 tablespoons (60 ml) oil to coat a 9 by 13-inch (23 by 33 cm) baking dish. With oiled hands, gently punch down the dough, then gather the edges of the dough and pull into the middle, rotating the bowl as you go. Turn the dough over and transfer to the prepared baking dish.

Gently guide the dough into the corners, but do not force it. As the gluten relaxes during the second rise, the dough will become easier to handle. Cover the pan loosely with a kitchen towel and allow the dough to rise in a warm place until doubled in size, about 2 hours.

Preheat the oven to 450°F (230°C) with the rack set in the center.

With oiled fingers, dimple the focaccia all over the surface, making very deep indentations almost all the way through the dough. Sprinkle it with 1 cup (100 g) Parmesan and the black pepper, then a generous pinch of flaky salt.

Bake until the dough is puffed and the cheese is deep golden brown, about 15 minutes. Remove from the oven, drizzle with a tablespoon of oil, sprinkle with the remaining cheese, cover with foil, and continue to bake until the focaccia is cooked through, about 10 minutes longer.

Remove from the oven and let cool for 15 minutes. Lift out of the pan, top with more Parmesan, slice, and serve warm with oil for dipping.

Makes 1 loaf

1 envelope active dry yeast

3 teaspoons granulated sugar

2½ cups (600 ml) water, warmed to 115°F (46°C)

1½ pounds (680 g) bread flour

1½ tablespoons kosher salt

5 tablespoons plus 4 tablespoons (135 ml) extra-virgin olive oil, plus more for oiling hands, topping, and serving

1 cup (100 g) plus ¼ cup (25 g) freshly grated Parmesan cheese, plus more for topping

2 teaspoons freshly ground black pepper

Pinch flaky salt

Best Ever Bolognese

I promised the Ultimates, and with this recipe, I'm truly delivering.
It's the meatiest meat sauce mixed with, wait for it, creamy béchamel.
If you can get your hands on some fresh pasta to serve this with, do it.
Either way you'll feel like you're in Italy eating at Nonna's house.

Serves 6 to 8

FOR THE BÉCHAMEL:

4 tablespoons unsalted butter

4 tablespoons all-purpose flour

2⅔ cups (630 ml) milk

1 cup (100 g) freshly grated
   Parmesan cheese

Kosher salt and freshly ground pepper

FOR THE RAGÙ:

3 tablespoons extra-virgin olive oil

3 ounces (85 g) pancetta,
   finely chopped

1 onion, finely diced

3 medium stalks celery with leaves,
   finely diced

3 small carrots, finely diced

6 cloves garlic, roughly chopped

10 ounces (280 g) ground pork

10 ounces (280 g) ground beef

2 tablespoons tomato paste

⅔ cup (165 ml) dry red wine

1 cup (240 ml) half-and-half,
   heavy cream, or milk

1 (28-ounce/795 g) can San
   Marzano tomatoes

Kosher salt and freshly ground
   black pepper

FOR SERVING:

1 to 2 pounds (455 to 910 g) cooked
   fresh garganelli pasta or any other
   pasta of your choosing

Side of Basil Pesto (page 234)
   and Burrata cheese (optional)

TO MAKE THE BÉCHAMEL: In a large saucepan, melt the butter over medium-high heat. Add the flour and cook, stirring with a whisk, for 3 minutes. Slowly add the milk and whisk together. Add the grated Parmesan and salt and pepper. Whisk and cook over medium heat for several minutes, until slightly thickened. Remove from heat and let cool.

TO MAKE THE RAGÙ: In a 12-inch (30.5 cm) Dutch oven, heat the oil over medium-high heat. Add the pancetta, onion, celery, and carrots and sauté, stirring frequently with a wooden spoon, about 10 minutes. Add the garlic and sauté for 30 seconds before adding the pork and beef. Stir the meats into the pancetta and vegetables and slowly brown over medium heat, breaking them up with a wooden spoon. Stir often for about 15 minutes, or until the meats are a deep brown. Add the tomato paste and stir to combine.

Pour the wine into the Dutch oven, lowering the heat so the sauce bubbles quietly. Stir occasionally until the wine has reduced by half, about 3 minutes. Scrape up the brown bits as the wine bubbles. Stir in the half-and-half. Adjust the heat so the liquid bubbles very slowly. Partially cover the pot and cook for 30 minutes. Stir frequently to check for sticking. Add the tomatoes, crushing them with your hands as they go into the pot. Cook uncovered at a very slow bubble for another 20 to 30 minutes, or until the sauce resembles a thick, meaty stew. Season with salt and pepper.

TO SERVE: Once cooked, stir the béchamel sauce into the meat sauce with a wooden spoon until fully combined. Add the cooked fresh pasta and stir to combine. Optional: Add the spoonful of pesto or burrata on top, if you want to be extra.

Lemon Poached Chicken + Rice with Thai Chimichurri

Once upon a time in Portland, my best friend Matt and I went on a food truck crawl. Our favorite bite, hands down, was the poached chicken and rice from Nong's Khao Man Gai. It was bright and zingy and loaded with Thai flavors, which I've done my very best to recreate so I can have it anytime I want. If you have the opportunity to try this dish IRL, I strongly encourage you to do so!! But until then, this easy homemade version will still rock your world.

Make the Thai chimichurri according to the instructions. Set aside while you poach the chicken.

In a large pot, place the chicken, lemons, salt, garlic, and peppercorns and cover with at least 2 inches (5 cm) of room temperature water.

Place the pot over medium-high heat and bring to a boil. Once the water is boiling, reduce heat, cover, and simmer until the internal temperature of the chicken reaches 165°F (74°C) on an instant-read thermometer, 10 to 20 minutes, based on the thickness of the chicken breasts.

Use tongs to remove the chicken breasts from the water. Discard the cooking water, lemons, garlic, and peppercorns.

TO SERVE: Thinly slice the chicken and serve over the rice. Spoon the Thai chimichurri and chili crisp over the chicken, then serve alongside the sliced cucumber and fresh Thai basil.

Serves 4

1 recipe Thai-Style Chimichurri (page 231)
3 large boneless, skinless chicken breasts, patted dry
1 tablespoon kosher salt
3 lemons, thinly sliced
3 cloves garlic, smashed
2 teaspoons whole black peppercorns

FOR SERVING:
4 cups (516 g) steamed white jasmine rice
¼ cup chili crisp
1 cup sliced cucumbers
¼ to ½ cup (13 to 25 g) fresh Thai basil

The Perfect *Fried* Chicken Sammy

I don't usually do a whole lot of deep-frying, mostly because I think there are better ways to give a dish a ton of great flavor. But for the perfect fried chicken sandwich, I will gladly make an exception. This sandwich—in all its messy, spicy, sweet perfection—will put any fried chicken joint to shame. I like to think of it as the ultimate Sunday sandwich, best served up with plenty of hot sauce and pickles.

Serves 4

FOR THE SPECIAL SAUCE:

½ cup (120 ml) plus 2 tablespoons mayonnaise

¼ cup (60 ml) honey

3 tablespoons yellow mustard

¼ cup (60 ml) barbecue sauce

2 teaspoons fresh lemon juice or pickle juice

Pinch kosher salt

FOR THE FRIED CHICKEN:

4 boneless, skinless chicken thighs

2 teaspoons plus 2½ teaspoons kosher salt, plus more for seasoning

1 cup (240 ml) buttermilk

2 to 4 teaspoons hot sauce (depending on desired spice level), plus more for serving

1 cup (125 g) all-purpose flour

½ cup (65 g) cornstarch

2 teaspoons baking powder

2 teaspoons garlic powder

2 teaspoons paprika

1 teaspoon freshly ground black pepper

4 cups (960 ml) canola oil, for frying

FOR ASSEMBLING:

4 brioche or potato buns, lightly toasted with butter

Bread-and-butter pickles

Hot sauce

Arugula

TO MAKE THE SAUCE: In a small bowl, stir together the mayo, honey, mustard, barbecue sauce, and lemon or pickle juice until smooth. Season with salt and set aside.

TO MAKE THE FRIED CHICKEN: Pat the chicken thighs dry with paper towels and season generously with salt. Set aside.

In a large bowl, whisk together the buttermilk with the hot sauce and 2 teaspoons kosher salt.

In another large bowl, whisk together the flour, cornstarch, baking powder, garlic powder, paprika, 2½ teaspoons kosher salt, and pepper. Set aside.

When ready to fry, fill a large, heavy-bottomed pot with the canola oil. Heat to 350°F (175°C).

Working with one piece of chicken at a time, dip the chicken in the flour mixture to coat, then place in the buttermilk, covering to submerge. Allow excess to drip off, then dredge in the flour mixture again, pressing the flour into the chicken. Shake off excess.

Working in batches if necessary, carefully transfer the chicken to the oil and cook until it is crispy and deeply golden, and the internal temperature reaches 170°F (77°C) on an instant-read thermometer, 3 to 5 minutes per side, depending on the size of the thighs. Transfer to a plate lined with a paper towel and sprinkle with salt.

TO ASSEMBLE: Spread a generous amount of sauce on the bottom of each toasted bun, then top with pickles, a fried chicken thigh, lots more sauce, a few dashes of hot sauce, and a small handful of arugula. Top with the other half of the bun and serve.

Oven-Baked Ratatouille

Yes, as in the movie with the same name and the dish that has the ability to bring you to tears. I made this dish for Poppy when she was seven months old, and we've all been obsessed ever since. You take all your end-of-summer produce, toss it on a sheet pan, and roast it low and slow until everything reduces down into jammy, caramelized oblivion. Serve it with Basil Vinaigrette over polenta, chicken, salmon, rice—you name it. I dare you not to cry over how good it is.

TO MAKE THE RATATOUILLE: Preheat the oven 350°F (175°C).

On two large sheet pans, combine the eggplant, zucchini, onions, tomatoes, oil, and oregano and season with the salt and pepper. Toss to combine. Transfer to the oven and bake for 90 minutes to 2 hours, until jammy. Remove from the oven.

TO MAKE THE POLENTA: While the ratatouille bakes, in a large saucepan over medium heat, bring the milk to a simmer. Slowly whisk in the semolina flour. Continue whisking until thickened, about 2 minutes. If too thick, continue to add milk until you get the desired consistency. Remove from heat and stir in the butter until it melts, then stir in the mascarpone and Parmesan. Season with salt and pepper.

Serve the ratatouille over a bowl of polenta with fresh basil and thyme to garnish, and with a drizzle of basil vinaigrette to finish.

Serves 6 to 8

FOR THE RATATOUILLE:
6 cups (480 g) cubed eggplant
3 cups (345 g) cubed zucchini
2 cups (110 g) cubed onions
6 cups (870 g) cherry tomatoes, halved
¾ cup (180 ml) extra-virgin olive oil
1 teaspoon dried oregano
Kosher salt and freshly cracked pepper
Basil Vinaigrette (page 235)

FOR THE POLENTA:
3 cups (720 ml) whole milk, plus more as needed
1 cup (180 g) semolina flour
4 tablespoons unsalted butter
6 ounces (170 g) mascarpone cheese
4 ounces (115 g) freshly grated Parmesan cheese
Fresh thyme or basil for garnish

Slow-Roasted Side of Salmon

Ever since I discovered that the best way to cook fish is in the oven (i.e., it cooks more evenly, there's no more babysitting it on the stove, and there's less fishy oil splattered all over your cooktop), I've been a major fan of all the ways you can make impressive fish dishes with minimal effort. This one definitely checks those boxes and rewards you with tender, juicy salmon every time.

Serves 4 to 6

1 (2-pound/910 g) center-cut
  side of salmon (skin removed)
Kosher salt and freshly ground
  black pepper
1 lemon, thinly sliced
1 orange, thinly sliced
3 shallots, thinly sliced
¾ cup (115 g) Castelvetrano olives,
  pitted and halved
¾ cup (180 ml) extra-virgin olive oil
Fresh parsley, for serving
Flaky salt, for serving

Dry off the salmon and season with kosher salt and pepper.

Preheat the oven to 275°F (135°C). In a large, shallow baking dish combine the lemon, orange, shallots, and olives. Drizzle with half the oil and season with salt and pepper.

Place the salmon on top, and pour the remaining oil over the top.

Roast the salmon in the middle of the oven until tender and cooked through, about 40 minutes for medium-rare.

Top the salmon with parsley and flaky salt before serving.

NOTE: The cut of salmon counts here; make sure you're getting center-cut and skinless.

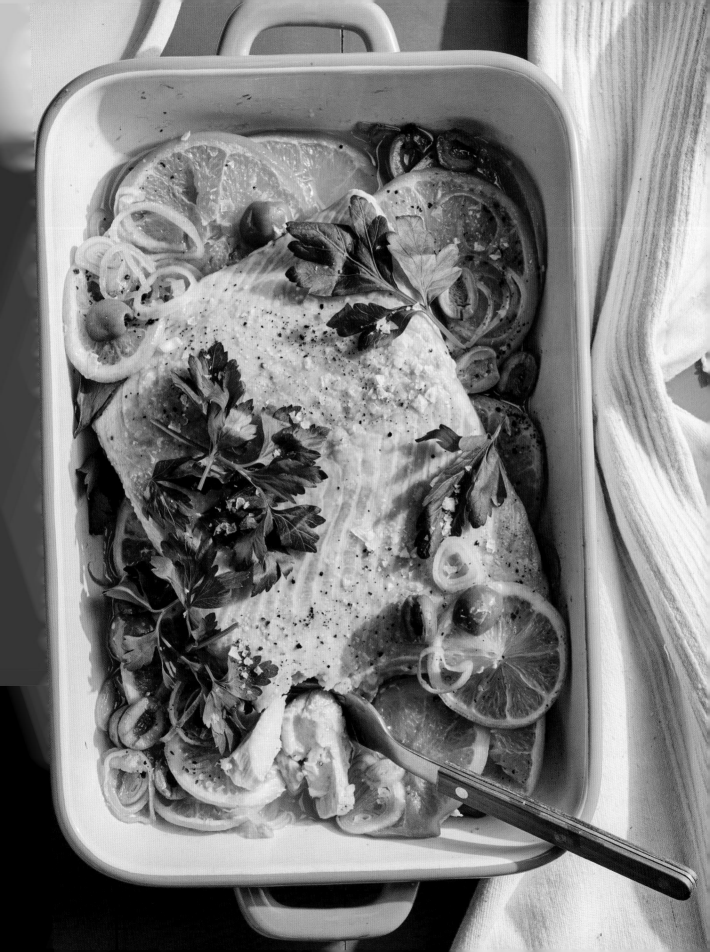

The Perfect
Steak

I'm a big believer that you are perfectly capable of making restaurant-quality food without needing a culinary degree. This recipe is proof of that— yes, you can make the PERFECT steak. And I do mean perfect. Cooking it doesn't require more than searing the meat in a pan, but what really puts it over the top is basting it with butter, rosemary, and garlic cloves.

Bring the steak to room temperature. Dry off the steak with paper towels and liberally season with salt and pepper.

Warm the oil in a cast-iron skillet over high heat. Once the oil is smoking, place the steak in the pan. Cook, without moving, until a deep crust forms, about 3 minutes. Flip and continue to cook until a crust forms on the other side. Use tongs to hold the steak upright, searing the sides, including the fat cap, until nice and browned.

Lay the steak down in the skillet and add the butter, garlic cloves, and rosemary. While tilting the pan, begin basting the steak with the butter, garlic, and rosemary, placing the garlic and rosemary on the top of the steak if they begin to burn. Baste for 30 to 60 seconds.

Transfer to a cutting board and allow to rest for 10 minutes. Slice and sprinkle with flake salt. Serve immediately.

Serves 1 to 2,
depending on how hungry you are

3 tablespoons canola oil
1 (8-ounce/225 g) bone-in
   rib eye steak
Kosher salt and freshly ground
   black pepper
3 tablespoons unsalted butter
5 cloves garlic, crushed with skins on
4 sprigs rosemary
Flaky salt, for serving

NOTE: I call for bone-in rib eye here, but boneless would work just as well.
You just don't have the visual wow factor of the bone.

Cajun Shrimp Pasta with Adam's Cajun Butter Sauce

Adam, one of my best friends and food stylist extraordinaire, is a culinary mastermind. He can do no wrong. So when he makes an epic Cajun shrimp party, you take notes. This pasta might be a little extra, but then again, so is Adam.

Serves 4 to 6

FOR THE SAUCE:

20 cloves garlic, skins removed

½ large yellow onion, roughly chopped

1½ teaspoons paprika

1½ teaspoons black pepper

1½ teaspoons cayenne pepper

1½ teaspoons onion powder

1½ teaspoons dry oregano

1½ teaspoons chili powder

1½ teaspoon Cajun spice mix

2 teaspoons Old Bay Seasoning

1 teaspoon crushed red pepper

1 cup (225 g/2 sticks) unsalted butter

2 tablespoons fresh lemon juice

1½ teaspoons Worcestershire sauce

1 teaspoon vinegar-based hot sauce

2 tablespoons brown sugar

FOR THE SHRIMP PASTA:

12 ounces (340 g) bucatini pasta

3 ears fresh corn, 1 sliced into ¾-inch (2 cm) coins, 2 stripped of kernels (1 cup/145 g)

8 ounces (225 g) andouille sausage or other smoked sausage, sliced

1 pound (455 g) extra-large shrimp, peeled and deveined

2 tablespoons chopped chives

Old Bay Seasoning

1 pound (455 g) king crab, legs split and heated in the oven at 350°F (175°C) for 15 min (optional)

Grilled or toasted bread, for serving

TO MAKE THE SAUCE: In a small food processor, pulse the garlic and onion until minced. Set aside.

Combine the paprika, black pepper, cayenne pepper, onion powder, oregano, chili powder, Cajun spice, Old Bay, and crushed red pepper in a bowl. In a large skillet over medium heat, melt the butter, add in the minced garlic and onions, and cook for about 4 minutes, until fragrant. Add the lemon juice, Worcestershire sauce, hot sauce, and brown sugar. Stir together until fully combined.

Add in the dry spices and let the mixture come to a boil, stirring often until combined, about 5 minutes. Remove the sauce from the heat and place in a bowl until ready to combine with the pasta.

TO MAKE THE SHRIMP PASTA: Cook the pasta according to the package instructions, reserving ½ cup (120 ml) of the pasta water to thin the sauce later if needed. After removing the pasta from the water, blanche the corn coins in the same pot of water for 4 minutes. Remove from the water and reserve.

In a large skillet, sauté the sausage over medium-high heat until nicely browned, about 5 minutes. Add in the shrimp and continue to cook, turning the shrimp occasionally, until the shrimp is cooked through, about 4 minutes. Add the corn coins and corn kernels and continue to cook for 2 minutes more.

Pour the reserved sauce over the shrimp and sausage and return to a simmer over medium heat. Add the pasta to the sauce and stir to combine, thinning with the reserved pasta water if needed. Top with the chives, a sprinkle of Old Bay, and king crab legs (if using) and serve with the grilled bread.

Chicken with Spanish Romesco

Herby Roasted

I'm going to level with you: If you're going to roast an entire chicken, then you best be spatchcocking it. By using kitchen shears to trim out the backbone (easy peasy, I promise) and flattening out the whole bird, you cut down on the roasting time and get even cooking. Plus, once you get the hang of it, you'll feel like a total boss, especially when you serve your expertly cooked chicken with a smoky, peppery, creamy Spanish romesco sauce.

Preheat the oven to 350°F (175°C) and line a sheet pan with foil or parchment. In a small bowl, combine the butter, oregano, rosemary, and lemon zest.

TO SPATCHCOCK THE CHICKEN: Using poultry shears, cut along each side of the backbone and remove it. Turn the chicken breast side up and press on the breastbone to flatten the chicken. Carefully work your fingers under the skin of each area facing up, clearing the way for the butter. If you need to make small nicks on the skin to allow for the butter, that's fine. Divide the butter mixture into 5 equal balls and stuff 1 ball under each thigh and each breast, working it around gently to make an even layer across all the meat. Take the remaining ball and divide it to stuff inside the wings.

TO ROAST THE CHICKEN: Drizzle the oil and season with salt on both sides of the chicken. Place the chicken skin side up on the sheet pan and roast for 30 minutes.

Increase the oven temperature to 425°F (220°C) and roast the chicken until golden brown, with the thighs cooked to 155°F (68°C) when read with an instant-read thermometer, another 20 to 25 minutes. To crisp up the skin, set the oven to broil and cook until the skin is crispy with some charred spots, another 5 to 8 minutes. Keep an eye on it because broilers vary dramatically! Remove from the oven and let rest for 15 to 20 minutes before serving on a platter, with the romesco sauce alongside. Garnish the platter with an abundance of parsley, rosemary, oregano, and fresh lemon slices. Then sit back and take in the compliments.

Serves 3 to 4

- ½ cup (115 g/1 stick) unsalted butter, softened
- 1 tablespoon finely minced fresh oregano, plus torn leaves for garnish
- 1 tablespoon finely minced fresh rosemary, plus torn sprigs for garnish
- 2 lemons, 1 zested and 1 sliced
- 1 (5 pound/2.3 kg) chicken, spatchcocked
- ¼ cup (60 ml) extra-virgin olive oil
- 1 tablespoon sea salt
- Romesco Sauce (page 232), at room temperature
- Torn fresh parsley, for garnish

NOTE: Making the romesco sauce ahead gives the flavors time to develop. Making it one day ahead or the morning of a gathering works best.

Pizza, Pasta
+ a Few Other Carbs

From the very beginning, this has been a featured chapter in my cookbooks. It's kind of a big fat duh because carbs are my favorite food group, and I'm willing to bet that they're yours too. What's not to love about all that starchy, hearty, belly-filling goodness? Whether we're talking pizza, pasta, bread, or any other carb cousin, they're the perfect blank canvases to load up with flavor. And while, yes, my favorite accompaniment for all the carbs is a pair of stretchy pants—because these recipes, like all my favorite dishes, strike the perfect balance between fresh and light and downright indulgent— these won't leave you feeling like you need to take a nap. (Though, there's no judgment if you do!)

Meaty
Mascarpone Pasta

Is it a cozy blanket? A warm hug? No, it's just the creamiest, meatiest bowl of pasta you could ever want. Make this anytime you have a bad day.

Serves 6

8 ounces (225 g) diced pancetta

1½ pounds (680 g) mild Italian sausage, casings removed

Extra-virgin olive oil, as needed

1 yellow onion, diced

4 cloves garlic, diced

1 (16-ounce/455 g) jar roasted red peppers, drained and diced

2 tablespoons tomato paste

Kosher salt and freshly ground black pepper

2 (15-ounce/425 g) cans crushed tomatoes

4 tablespoons unsalted butter, cut into 4 pieces

8 ounces (225 g) mascarpone, plus more for topping

2 cups (200 g) freshly grated Parmesan cheese, plus more for topping

2 teaspoons crushed red pepper, plus more as desired

1 pound (455 g) short noodle pasta, such as garganelli or shells

Heat a large high-rimmed skillet over medium-high heat and cook the pancetta, stirring occasionally, until the pancetta is lightly golden and the fat begins to render, about 6 minutes. Use a slotted spoon to transfer to a plate, then cook the sausage in the skillet, stirring occasionally, until no pink remains, about 8 minutes. Transfer to the plate with the pancetta.

If needed, pour 2 tablespoons of oil into the skillet. Reduce heat to medium, then add the onion and cook until softened, stirring occasionally, about 10 minutes. Add the garlic and cook while stirring for 1 more minute. Stir in the red peppers and tomato paste, and season with salt and black pepper.

Add the crushed tomatoes and butter and stir, then bring the mixture to a boil over high heat. Return the pancetta and sausage to the skillet. Reduce the heat to medium and cook, stirring occasionally, to allow the flavors to meld. The sauce will reduce slightly after about 20 minutes. Adjust the heat to medium-low if the tomato sauce is reducing too much. Add the mascarpone and Parmesan. Season with salt, black pepper, and the crushed red pepper.

Meanwhile, bring a large pot of salted water to a boil. Drop in the pasta and cook according to package instructions. Transfer the pasta directly from the pasta water to the sauce and toss to coat. Season with salt and black pepper.

Top with more Parmesan, a few generous dollops of mascarpone, and more crushed red pepper if you choose. Serve immediately.

Pasta with Stracciatella

Tomato confit was the brainchild of Matt and Adam's good friend Dana. And I've been obsessed ever since being introduced, because it's actually genius how simple it is to cook down a pan of cherry tomatoes in olive oil and then end up with the best pasta sauce of all time. The only thing that improves this dish is serving it with creamy stracciatella, which is basically the inside of a ball of Burrata. So if you can't find stracciatella, use Burrata instead.

In a medium skillet, place the tomatoes and oil over medium-high heat. Season with salt and pepper. Give the mixture a stir to combine.

Once the oil starts to get hot and the tomatoes start to blister, reduce the heat to medium and let simmer for roughly 30 minutes, stirring every 10 minutes. After 30-ish minutes, the tomatoes should be falling apart. Remove them from the heat and let cool for a few minutes.

Meanwhile, bring a large pot of salted water to a boil. Add the pasta and cook until al dente. Reserve about ¼ cup (60 ml) of the pasta water once cooked and add it to the tomato confit along with the cheese and the cooked and drained pasta. Season with salt and at least 2 teaspoons of freshly cracked black pepper. Taste and adjust as needed before serving.

Serves 4 to 6

1 pound (455 g) cherry tomatoes, quartered
⅓ cup (75 ml) extra-virgin olive oil
Kosher salt and freshly cracked black pepper
1 pound (455 g) pasta
8 ounces (225 g) stracciatella cheese

Pasta with Peas + Pesto

When you want fresh, bright flavors bundled up in a bowl of pasta, do yourself a favor and make this dish. It's basically my favorite crostini topping in pasta form! Mama Dalkin, this one is for you.

Serves 4 to 6

4 cloves garlic, finely chopped
⅓ cup (30 g) finely grated Pecorino Romano cheese, plus more to finish
⅓ cup (75 ml) extra-virgin olive oil
2 lemons, 1 juiced and 1 thinly sliced
¼ teaspoon crushed red pepper
Kosher salt and freshly cracked black pepper
1 (10-ounce/280 g) package frozen peas, completely thawed
1 pound (455 g) pasta
Basil Pesto (page 234)
Fresh basil, for garnish

In a medium bowl, whisk together the garlic, Pecorino, oil, lemon juice, crushed red pepper, salt, and plenty of black pepper. Add the thawed peas and stir to combine. Taste and adjust salt and black pepper as needed. Use the back of a fork to just roughly mash half of the peas so they are a little chunkier, and leave the other half whole.

Meanwhile, bring a large pot of salted water to a boil and cook the pasta according to the package instructions. Drain and toss the pasta with the smashed peas and a few large spoonfuls of pesto. Top with the basil, lemon slices, and more salt and black pepper before serving.

Spaghetti
alla Nerano

This classic Italian pasta is similar to cacio e pepe, so already you know it's going to be amazing. But this time we're taking things one step further with the addition of lightly fried zucchini slices and a zip of lemon zest. The effect is similar to eating Med-side in sunny Positano, where this dish is legendary.

In a large skillet, heat 3 tablespoons of the oil over medium heat and add the garlic. Fry the zucchini in batches, until lightly golden around the edges, 3 to 4 minutes on each side. Transfer to a sheet pan lined with a paper towel and season with salt. Add more oil to the pan as needed and discard the garlic once golden. Keep the skillet and any oil left in the pan.

Bring a large pot of salted water to boil over high heat. Add the pasta to the water and cook until al dente, about 8 minutes. Reserve 3 cups (720 ml) of pasta water before draining.

Reheat the skillet over medium-high heat and return half the zucchini back to the pan with 2 cups (480 ml) of the reserved pasta water. Mash the zucchini up with a fork.

Set aside about ¾ cup (70 g) of the cheese for garnishing. In a medium bowl, stir together the cheese, zest, and pepper. Add the cooked pasta, cheese mixture, and butter to the skillet and stir to make a creamy sauce, adding more pasta water as needed to melt the cheese and coat the pasta. Transfer the pasta to a large platter and scatter the remaining fried zucchini, cheese, and torn basil over the top. Drizzle with a bit of oil and a few more grinds of pepper and serve.

Serves 4

½ cup (120 ml) extra-virgin olive oil, plus more for garnish

2 cloves garlic

4 small green zucchini, thinly sliced ⅛-inch (3 mm) wide

Kosher salt

1 pound (455 g) spaghetti

10 ounces (280 g) freshly grated Pecorino Romano cheese (see Note), plus more for serving

Zest of 1 lemon

1 teaspoon freshly ground black pepper, plus more for garnish

2 tablespoons unsalted butter

2 handfuls fresh basil, torn

NOTE: You'll want to grate your own cheese for this recipe instead of buying pre-grated, otherwise it'll clump up on you.

Thomas's Tri-Tip Sandwiches with Onions + Melted Cheese

There is nothing Thomas loves more in this life, other than me and Poppy, than a tri-tip sandwich. I can't blame him—tri-tip is unfussy, grills up to perfection, and is super flavorful. Plus it gets even more of a boost here from an all-around powerhouse rub and a slathering of barbecue sauce to keep things juicy. There's a reason why this is an important sandwich for us in the summer and ends up on the grill pretty much every other week.

Serves 4 to 6

FOR THE RUB:

2 tablespoons finely ground coffee

1½ tablespoons kosher salt

1½ tablespoons garlic powder

1 teaspoon freshly cracked black pepper

1 tablespoon brown sugar

½ teaspoon dried oregano

¼ teaspoon dried thyme

¼ teaspoon paprika

¼ teaspoon cayenne pepper

FOR THE SANDWICH:

1 (2-pound/910 g) whole tri-tip steak

4 tablespoons rub (see above)

Ciabatta rolls or Cacio e Pepe Focaccia (page 103)

Caramelized Onions (page 234)

½ pound (225 g) deli-sliced mozzarella

Barbecue sauce, for serving

TO MAKE THE RUB: In a medium bowl, combine the coffee, salt, garlic powder, black pepper, brown sugar, oregano, thyme, paprika, and cayenne pepper.

TO MAKE THE SANDWICH: Trim the silver skin off the tri-tip but leave some of the fat. Massage the meat with the rub until fully covered, and let rest at room temperature for 1 hour.

Prepare a charcoal grill or gas grill to high heat. Place the tri-tip on the grill and sear one side well, 6 to 7 minutes, making sure it doesn't burn. Rotate the tri-tip, flip, and sear the other side for about the same amount of time. Reduce heat to medium-high or move the meat to a part of the grill that's not over direct flames. Rotate the meat again and cook for another 8 to 10 minutes. Flip and cook again for an additional 5 to 6 minutes. A 2-pound (910 g) roast will need 20 to 25 minutes total cooking time. Cook until an instant-read thermometer reads 120°F (49°C) for a rare roast, 130°F (54°C) for medium-rare, and 140°F (60°C) for medium.

Let the meat rest on a cutting board for 10 to 20 minutes to allow the juice to redistribute.

To serve, slice the tri-tip against the grain. Grill the ciabatta rolls, slather them with caramelized onions and barbecue sauce, then top the bread with the sliced tri-tip and plenty of cheese. Broil to melt cheese and top with the remaining bread. Serve warm.

Herby Orzo

You'd be hard-pressed to find a recipe that yields such big results from such easy prep. It honestly puts all other orzo recipes to shame and is my new favorite go-to for all things side dish, potluck, and picnic.

Cook the orzo according to the package instructions. Drain and transfer the pasta into a serving bowl.

Reserve ¼ cup (40 g) of the feta. Crumble the remaining feta cheese directly into the orzo, add the basil vinaigrette and lemon juice, and toss to combine. Season with salt and pepper.

Add in fresh mint, basil, and chives and stir to combine. Garnish with extra feta and herbs on top.

Serves 4 to 6

1 pound (455 g) orzo pasta
1 cup (150 g) feta cheese
1 cup (240 ml) Basil Vinaigrette (page 235)
Juice of 1 lemon
Kosher salt and freshly ground black pepper
¼ cup (8 g) fresh mint, torn
¼ cup (8 g) fresh basil, torn
¼ cup (8 g) fresh chives, finely chopped

Castelvetrano & Artichoke
Pizza with Shaved Parm

I pulled out all the stops for this pie, which is a mind-bending combo of salty, spicy, and cheesy, plus the perfect amount of sweet from shallots that are cooked down to a jammy confit. I round things out with Castelvetrano olives, which deserve to be on anything good in this world. I mean, it's full-on obsession-worthy.

Serves 4 to 6

FOR THE SHALLOT CONFIT:

¼ cup (60 ml) extra-virgin olive oil

6 to 8 shallots, trimmed, cleaned, and thinly sliced

2 teaspoons kosher salt

1 teaspoon freshly cracked black pepper

4 cloves garlic, thinly sliced

FOR THE PIZZA:

All-purpose flour, for dusting

1 pound (455 g) of your favorite pizza dough, divided in half

1 to 2 cups (110 to 220 g) freshly shredded Gruyère cheese

1 large ball of fresh mozzarella, torn into pieces

1 cup (155 g) pitted Castelvetrano olives, smashed/torn in half

½ cup (75 g) canned artichoke hearts, drained, patted dry, and quartered

Kosher salt and freshly cracked black pepper

Crushed red pepper

Plenty of freshly shaved Parmesan cheese

1 lemon

TO MAKE THE CONFIT: In a large deep saucepan, heat the oil over medium heat until it shimmers. Add the shallots, season with the salt and black pepper, and cook, stirring occasionally, until the edges begin to brown, 5 to 7 minutes. Be careful not to allow them to burn.

Reduce the heat to low, cover, and cook, stirring occasionally, until the shallots are completely softened and somewhat translucent, 15-ish minutes. Uncover and reduce the heat to the lowest setting on your stove. Add the garlic and cook for 3 to 4 minutes over low heat. Transfer to a container and set aside.

TO MAKE THE PIZZA: Preheat the oven to 475°F (245°C) with a pizza stone in the top third of the oven if available.

On a lightly floured surface, roll each portion of the dough thin. Transfer each one to an oiled sheet pan and flatten out to 8 to 10 inches (20 to 25 cm) in diameter, using a rolling pin. If you are using a pizza stone instead, sprinkle some flour on a pizza peel and place the stretched-out dough on the peel.

Once your 2 pizza doughs are flat and ready to be heated, use a spoon to spread about ¼ cup (60 ml) of the shallot confit all around each portion of the dough, leaving a 1-inch (2.5 cm) border for the crust.

Top each pizza with half of the shredded Gruyère, followed by half the fresh mozzarella, olives, and artichokes, and season with salt, black pepper, and crushed red pepper. Transfer a baking sheet with one of the pizzas to the oven, or use the peel to slide a pizza onto the preheated pizza stone. Bake for 12 to 13 minutes, until the crust is perfect.

Remove the pizza from the oven. Adjust seasoning as needed, add tons of shaved Parmesan, squeeze lemon juice on top, and serve. Repeat with the other pizza.

BLT

Chopped Salad Pizza

Ever wonder what would happen if you took all of your favorite fixings from a BLT and sprinkled them over a pizza? Oh, pretty much just the freshest and most flavorful pie you can imagine. I added extra cheese here too, because obviously.

Serves 4 to 6

- All-purpose flour, for dusting
- 1 pound (455 g) of your favorite pizza dough, divided in half
- 4 tablespoons extra-virgin olive oil, plus more for sheet pans
- 2 cups (460 g) fresh mozzarella cheese, torn
- ½ teaspoon crushed red pepper
- 8 slices center-cut bacon, cooked and torn
- 1 cup (145 g) halved cherry tomatoes
- 1 cup (145 g) raw corn, sliced from the cob
- 1 cup (55 g) shredded romaine lettuce
- ½ cup (75 g) feta cheese
- Kosher salt and freshly cracked black pepper
- ½ cup (120 ml) Cilantro Vinaigrette (page 235)

Preheat the oven to 475°F (245°C) with a pizza stone in the top third of the oven if available.

On a lightly floured surface, roll each portion of the dough thin. Transfer each one to an oiled sheet pan and flatten out to 8 to 10 inches (20 to 25 cm) in diameter, using a rolling pin. Transfer a baking sheet with one of the pizzas to the oven, or use the peel to slide a pizza onto the preheated pizza stone. Drizzle each pizza with oil and top with half the mozzarella and crushed red pepper. Bake for 8 to 12 minutes until the crust is deep golden brown.

Remove the pizza from the oven and top with half of the bacon, tomatoes, corn, romaine, and feta. Season with salt and black pepper and a drizzle of cilantro vinaigrette. Serve immediately. Repeat with the second pizza.

Chorizo Fontina Basil Pizza

This is my play on an old-school sausage pizza, almost like its cooler younger sister. It's got extra-melty Fontina cheese and smoky chorizo, plus charred onions thrown in for good measure. Add some basil oil and you're in business.

Serves 4 to 6

FOR THE CHORIZO:

2 tablespoons extra-virgin olive oil
10 ounces (280 g) ground chorizo
1 onion, thinly sliced

FOR THE BASIL OIL:

1 clove garlic
½ cup (20 g) packed fresh
    basil leaves
¼ cup (60 ml) plus 1 tablespoon
    extra-virgin olive oil
Kosher salt and freshly ground
    black pepper

FOR THE PIZZA:

All-purpose flour, for dusting
1 pound (455 g) of your favorite
    pizza dough, halved
Olive oil, for greasing the sheet pans
½ cup (120 ml) your favorite red
    pizza sauce
1½ cups (160 g) shredded
    Fontina cheese
Fresh basil, for garnish

TO PREPARE THE CHORIZO: In a large skillet over medium-high heat, warm the oil. Add the chorizo and cook until browned, breaking up the sausage with a wooden spoon as you go, about 4 minutes. Transfer to a plate using a slotted spoon. Add the onion to the pan and stir to pick up oil or leftover bits from the chorizo. Cook the onions until softened and charred, about 8 minutes. Set aside to cool.

TO MAKE THE BASIL OIL: With a small food processor running, drop the garlic clove through the feed tube to mince. Stop the processor and add the basil. Pulse until finely chopped. Then add the oil and season with salt and pepper. Pulse to combine.

TO MAKE THE PIZZA: Preheat an oven to 500°F (260°C) with a pizza stone in the top third of the oven if available.

On a lightly floured surface, stretch 1 portion of the dough to an 8 to 10-inch (20 to 25 cm) round.

Transfer to a greased baking sheet or a lightly floured pizza peel if you are using a pizza stone. Spread half the pizza sauce over the dough, leaving a 1-inch (2.5 cm) border for the crust. Then sprinkle with half the cheese and half the chorizo and onion mixture.

Transfer a baking sheet with one of the pizzas to the oven, or use the peel to slide a pizza onto the preheated pizza stone. Bake until the cheese is bubbling and the crust is deep golden brown, 8 to 10 minutes. Allow to cool for 3 minutes, then drizzle with some basil oil and garnish with fresh basil leaves. Repeat with remaining ingredients and serve the pizzas immediately.

Cacio e Pepe
Flatbread

It's not often that I'm at a loss for words, but after trying this perfectly salty, cheesy, doughy bread, I got nothin'. All I can say is that I want to live in a world where this flows like a waterfall, maybe next to a waterfall of wine, because that's all you need in order to call this a meal.

Preheat an oven set with a pizza stone in the upper third to 500°F (260°C).

On a lightly floured surface, stretch 1 portion of the dough to an 8 to 10-inch (20 to 25 cm) round. Transfer to a lightly floured pizza peel.

Cover the dough with half of the Pecorino and Parmesan, then place half of the mozzarella toward the center of the pizza, leaving a 1-inch (2.5 cm) crust. Add a light drizzle of oil and a few very generous grinds of pepper. Transfer to the oven and bake on the pizza stone until the cheese is bubbling and the crust is deep golden brown, about 10 minutes. Allow to cool slightly, then top with more Parmesan. Repeat with remaining ingredients and serve immediately.

Serves 4 to 6

All-purpose flour, for dusting
1 pound (455 g) of your favorite pizza dough, halved
1 cup (100 g) freshly grated Pecorino Romano
½ cup (50 g) freshly grated Parmesan, plus more for serving
4 ounces (115 g) mozzarella di bufala, drained, dried, and thinly sliced
Extra-virgin olive oil, for drizzling
Freshly ground black pepper

Italian Dinner Party

Full menu serves 4 to 6

I find so much inspiration when I'm abroad, so you can imagine how much I missed my usual trips around the world during the past couple years. Since we weren't visiting any of my favorite locales or checking new ones off my bucket list, I did the next best thing: I brought them to me. After Thomas and I moved into our new house, we did countless Italian nights. It may not have been Rome or Positano IRL, but all the carbs, steaks, and wine really did transport us back to one of our favorite places on the planet.

Besides giving me major Italia vibes, what I love about this menu is that it can mostly be prepped in advance so that you can actually enjoy your own party. The fig and prosciutto appetizer is beyond easy, the individual tiramisus can be made ahead, and there's nothing to the salad and pasta, but they're all wildly delish. Even the steak can be made ahead and just seared (Hello, reverse sear technique!) when the guests arrive, which means you won't have to sweat cooking it to the perfect doneness. And the Negroni Spritzes can be batched out then topped off with sparkling water when you're ready for your first round. So go ahead, take a load off. *Mangia!*

Negroni Spritz

2 cups (480 ml) freshly squeezed orange juice
   (from 3 to 4 oranges)
1 cup (240 ml) Campari
1 cup (240 ml) gin
1 cup (240 ml) sweet vermouth
2 to 3 cups (480 to 720 ml) club soda
Thin orange slices, for serving

In a large glass measuring cup or pitcher, stir together
the orange juice, Campari, gin, and vermouth until well
combined. Stir in the club soda. Fill four to six glasses
with ice and divide the drink mixture among them.
Garnish with a slice of orange and serve.

Figs with Prosciutto

2 to 3 pints (580 to 870 g) fresh figs
   (Make sure they are mostly soft—hard figs
   taste like cardboard.)
6 ounces (170 g) thinly sliced prosciutto
½ cup (50 g) freshly shaved Parmesan cheese
Drizzle of extra-virgin olive oil
Drizzle of balsamic vinegar
Baby basil, for garnish

Arrange everything on a large serving platter and serve
at the beginning of the night as an appetizer, with the
Negroni Spritz (above).

Arugula Salad

OG Italian

FOR THE SALAD:

8 ounces (225 g) wild arugula, rinsed and dried

¾ cup (70 g) freshly shaved Parmesan cheese

FOR THE DRESSING:

2 tablespoons fresh lemon juice

2 tablespoons champagne vinegar

6 to 8 tablespoons (90 to 120 ml) extra-virgin olive oil

2 cloves garlic, finely minced

1 shallot, finely minced

½ cup (50 g) freshly ground Parmesan cheese

Kosher salt and freshly cracked black pepper

TO ASSEMBLE THE SALAD: In a large shallow salad bowl, arrange the arugula and top with plenty of the shaved Parmesan.

TO MAKE THE DRESSING: In another bowl, whisk together all ingredients for the dressing and then drizzle on top of the arugula. Toss and serve.

Linguine
al Limone

In a large sauté pan, combine the zest of both lemons and the heavy cream. Bring the mixture to a simmer over medium heat and stir to combine. Reduce the heat to low and add the butter. Season with salt and pepper and whisk until smooth. Remove from heat.

Cook the pasta according to the package instructions until al dente. Reserve ½ to ¾ cup (120 to 180 ml) of the pasta water before draining and set aside. Drain the pasta and then transfer it into the lemon cream sauce along with the Parmesan.

Add ¼ cup (60 ml) pasta cooking liquid to the lemon cream sauce and return to medium heat—that should be enough to thin it out. If it's still too thick, add a few more tablespoons of the reserved pasta water until smooth. Toss the pasta in the lemon sauce until the cheese melts and the pasta is evenly coated. Add the lemon juice, adjust salt and pepper as needed, and serve.

Zest and juice of 2 lemons

1 cup (240 ml) heavy cream

1½ pounds (680 g) fresh spaghetti or other long pasta

4 tablespoons unsalted butter

Kosher salt and freshly ground black pepper

1 cup (100 g) finely grated fresh Parmesan cheese

Florentine
Reverse Sear Steak

2 rib eye steaks, each about
 1½ pounds (680 g), 1½-inch
 (4 cm) thick
Kosher salt and freshly cracked
 black pepper
1 to 2 teaspoons extra-virgin olive oil

Liberally season both rib eyes with salt and pepper. You want a really good coating on both sides. Once seasoned, let the meat rest for an hour or two at room temperature.

Preheat the oven to 275°F (135°C).

Transfer the steaks onto a wire rack fitted on top of a sheet pan and place into the preheated oven.

If you're going for rare, cook for 20 to 25 minutes, until the internal temperature is 110°F (43°C) on an instant-read thermometer. If you're going for medium rare, cook for 25 to 30 minutes, until the internal temperature is 120°F (49°C). If you're going for medium, cook for 30 to 35 minutes, until the internal temperature is 125°F (52°C).

Once the steaks have been removed from the oven, heat a cast-iron skillet over high heat. Pour 1 to 2 teaspoons of oil into the skillet and carefully swirl around before the handle is hot. Sear the steaks, one at a time, for 2 to 3 minutes per side until you have a great golden crust. Feel free to move the steaks around as they are searing to get the most char possible. Remove the steaks from the skillet and let rest for 10 minutes before slicing.

Tiramisu
Trifles

In a bowl, whisk together the cocoa powder, espresso, and vanilla and set aside.

In a stand mixer or using a hand mixer, beat the egg yolks and sugar until pale and thick, about 5 minutes. Add the salt and mascarpone and continue to whip until smooth. Add the chilled cream and continue to whip until the mixture is light and creamy and can hold a soft peak.

Have six individual trifle glasses ready. Dunk each ladyfinger in the espresso mixture to absorb the liquid, break in half, and place a few of the broken lady fingers at the bottom of each glass. Top the first layer of cookies with half of the whipped mascarpone mixture (a few spoonfuls per glass). Dust with cocoa powder. Repeat for another layer and then finish by dusting the top with cocoa powder. Cover with plastic wrap and chill for at least 2 hours before serving.

¼ cup (25 g) Dutch-process cocoa powder, plus more for dusting

1 cup (240 ml) brewed espresso

1 tablespoon vanilla extract

5 large pasteurized egg yolks, cold

½ cup (100 g) granulated sugar

¼ teaspoon kosher salt

2 (8-ounce/225 g) tubs mascarpone cheese, chilled

1¾ cups (420 ml) heavy cream, chilled

2 to 3 dozen hard ladyfinger cookies

Sides

What's not to love about a side dish? Whether it's crispy and salty, creamy and gooey, or roasty and caramelized, having a perfectly flavored comple- ment to whatever else I'm eating is one of my favorite moments in a meal. The recipes in this chapter are ALL-NEW, meaning they've never made an appearance on my website or in any past cookbooks. And yet, they're so beloved that it's as though they've always been a part of the WGC rotation.

Crispy
Creamed Spinach

Throw away all your other creamed spinach recipes. This is the one.
The Fontina adds an extra layer of gooeyness in addition to the more traditional
cream cheese situation, and then the crispy panko topping just sends it over
the top. You'll want this one on the table for all the fall/winter dinner occasions.

Serves 4 to 6

¼ cup (60 ml) extra-virgin olive oil
3 pounds (1.4 kg) spinach
3 tablespoons unsalted butter
1 cup (80 g) panko bread crumbs
Kosher salt and freshly cracked
    black pepper
Zest and juice of 1 lemon
4 ounces (115 g) cream cheese,
    at room temperature
4 ounces (115 g) freshly grated
    Fontina cheese
¼ cup (60 ml) heavy cream

In a very large pot or Dutch oven, heat the oil over medium-high heat.
Add the spinach in batches, stirring and continuing to add as the spinach wilts.
Once wilted, cover the pot, reduce the heat to medium-low and continue
to cook, stirring every few minutes until the spinach is soft, 10 to 15 minutes.

While the spinach is cooking, melt the butter in a small skillet over medium-
high heat. Add the panko bread crumbs and season with salt, pepper, and
lemon zest. Stir and sauté until the bread crumbs are golden brown, about
3 minutes, and remove from the heat.

Break the cream cheese into small pieces and drop them into the Dutch
oven with the spinach, while still over low heat. Stir the cream cheese until
it's fully combined into the spinach. Add the Fontina, lemon juice, and heavy
cream and combine for about 1 minute until the Fontina is melted. Transfer
the spinach mixture to a serving bowl and sprinkle the toasted panko over
the top to serve.

Baby Sweet Potatoes
with Garlic Labneh + Romesco

Matt put it best: This is the only way sweet potatoes should ever be served. It's a little like patatas bravas—a spicy potato dish from Spain—but it brings in the complexity of the Japanese sweet potatoes. It is really simple, too, thanks to the combo of my easy garlic labneh and romesco sauces. This may just be my favorite side dish of all time.

Preheat the oven to 425°F (220°C).

Wash the potatoes well and pat dry. Poke holes all around each potato using a fork.

Rub the potatoes all over with the oil, then sprinkle liberally with salt and pepper. Place the potatoes on a sheet pan or aluminum foil and roast until tender when pierced with a fork, 40 to 45 minutes.

Transfer the potatoes to a plate and let cool for 10 minutes. Tear the sweet potatoes into large chunks and drizzle with plenty of the garlic labneh and romesco. Season with salt and serve.

Serves 4

4 to 6 small Japanese sweet potatoes
Extra-virgin olive oil
Kosher salt and freshly ground
   black pepper
1 recipe Garlic Labneh (page 234)
1 recipe Romesco Sauce (page 232)

NOTE: This is also excellent with a labneh and Basil Vinaigrette (page 235) combo.

Creamy
White Beans

A dish of creamy beans is a fall rite of passage in my book. It's also the perfect blank canvas to flavor up with cold-weather staples like rosemary and garlic, plus a spicy herb oil. Besides the beans' earthy deliciousness, the thing I love most about this dish is that it ages like a fine wine. You can make this a few days before your get-together and it will only get better. Add crusty bread and act like it took all day.

Serves 4 to 6

FOR THE BEANS:
12 ounces (340 g) dried cannellini beans
1 medium yellow onion, cut into wedges
5 cloves garlic, smashed
1 sprig rosemary
1 bay leaf
1 Calabrian chile
5 ounces (140 g) baby spinach
Sea salt

FOR THE SPICY HERB OIL:
½ cup (120 ml) extra-virgin olive oil
1 tablespoon fresh rosemary, minced
4 cloves garlic, thinly sliced
4 Calabrian chiles, thinly sliced, or ½ teaspoon red pepper flakes
1 teaspoon fennel seeds

Crusty bread, for serving

TO MAKE THE BEANS: Rinse the beans, put them into a large pot, and cover with cold water by 2 inches (5 cm). Add the onion, garlic, rosemary, bay leaf, and Calabrian chile. Bring the beans to a boil over high heat, then reduce to a high simmer. Skim off any foam during the cooking and discard. Cook until very tender, 50 to 60 minutes. Stir in the spinach and season with salt.

TO MAKE THE SPICY HERB OIL: While the beans are cooking, heat the oil in a small skillet or saucepan over medium-low heat. Add the rosemary, garlic, chiles, and fennel seeds. Cook until the garlic is lightly golden and the herbs and fennel are fragrant. Set aside.

TO ASSEMBLE AND SERVE: In a blender, puree about 2 cups (310 g) of the bean and spinach mixture briefly until smooth. Stir the puree back into the beans. Transfer the beans to a serving bowl, pour the spicy herb oil over the top, and serve with crusty bread.

Cheesy
Roasted Mushrooms

Similar to cooking eggplant, if you don't treat mushrooms properly, it's an issue. They get rubbery, mushy, and sad. Well, not in this recipe. Roasting the mushrooms with a healthy dose of cheesy stuffing keeps them tender, juicy, and caramelized to perfection. I especially love serving these alongside the Perfect Steak (page 115) or the Slow-Roasted Side of Salmon (page 112).

Preheat the oven to 425°F (220°C).

Place the torn mushrooms on a parchment-lined sheet pan. Drizzle with the oil and season with salt, black pepper, and crushed red pepper. Transfer the sheet pan into the oven and roast for 30 to 35 minutes until the mushrooms are fully cooked and the edges are crispy, tossing 15 minutes through.

Remove from the oven and sprinkle the cheeses on top.

Transfer the sheet pan back into the oven and roast for an additional 5 minutes until the cheese is fully melted. Remove the sheet pan from the oven, squeeze the lemon juice on top of the roasted mushrooms, and adjust salt and black pepper as needed. Serve immediately.

Serves 4 to 6

2 pounds (910 g) wild mushrooms, trimmed and torn into large pieces depending on size
¼ cup (60 ml) extra-virgin olive oil
Kosher salt and freshly cracked black pepper
1 teaspoon crushed red pepper
1 cup (100 g) freshly grated Parmesan cheese
1 cup (110 g) freshly shredded Gruyère cheese
Juice of 1 lemon

NOTE: You need ample room for roasting the mushrooms because otherwise they'll steam in the oven, and that's not what we're going for. If you find that your pan is too crowded and there's no space between the mushrooms, divide them between two sheet pans so you can achieve optimum crispy deliciousness.

Buffalo Cauliflower

There's a wildly expensive grocery store here in L.A. that makes some of the most insane Buffalo cauliflower I've ever had. (Hello Erewhon! I love you but I'll be broke if I shop there every week.) So instead of going there every time the craving strikes, I do myself (and my wallet) a favor by making my own version at home. The subtle heat playing off the creamy cauliflower with the crisped edges is so munch-worthy that this pretty much qualifies as a snack.

Serves 2 to 4

1 large head of cauliflower,
   cut into medium-size florets
1 tablespoon extra-virgin olive oil
1 tablespoon fresh lemon juice
½ teaspoon garlic powder
1 teaspoon kosher salt
1 teaspoon freshly cracked
   black pepper
½ cup (120 ml) Frank's RedHot
   Buffalo Wings Sauce, plus more
   for serving
2 tablespoons unsalted butter, melted
Garlic Labneh (page 234)
   or your fave blue cheese dressing,
   for serving

Preheat the oven to 425°F (220°C) and line a large sheet pan with parchment paper.

Transfer the cauliflower florets to a large bowl and toss with the oil, lemon juice, garlic powder, salt, and pepper. Spread the cauliflower in a single layer on the parchment-lined sheet pan and bake for 25 to 30 minutes, gently tossing the cauliflower halfway through cooking to ensure even roasting.

After 25 to 30 minutes, remove the sheet pan from the oven. In a small bowl, whisk together the hot sauce and melted butter. Turn the oven to broil. Pour the hot sauce mixture over the cauliflower florets and toss well to coat.

Return the sheet pan to the oven and broil for an additional 2 to 3 minutes, until extra crispy. Adjust seasoning as needed and serve with the garlic labneh.

Eggplant with Pesto

Sautéed

This might be the shortest recipe in the book, but it packs a big punch when it comes to flavor. That said, here's the deal: You gotta treat the eggplant right. Cook it improperly and it's pretty much soggy and worthless. BUT, load it up with olive oil and get a good sear on it, and you're in golden, beautiful business.

Heat a heavy-bottomed skillet over medium heat. Pour in the oil. Once the oil shimmers, add the eggplant chunks and season with salt and pepper. Sauté for 10 to 12 minutes until the eggplant is caramelized, tossing every few minutes as the sides start to turn golden brown.

Turn off the heat and carefully transfer the still-hot eggplant to a large bowl. Toss with the pesto while the eggplant is still warm so it semi-cooks the pesto's garlic and absorbs the cheese. Let rest for 10 minutes and then transfer to a serving dish. Scatter with more basil and serve.

Serves 2 to 4

¼ cup (60 ml) extra-virgin olive oil
1½ pounds (680 g) baby eggplant, cut into large 1½-inch (4 cm) coins
Kosher salt and freshly cracked black pepper
½ cup (120 ml) Basil Pesto (page 234)
Fresh basil, for serving

Brussels Sprouts + Brie Gratin

This dish is so fun, so different, and oh-so creamy, rich, and delicious that I decided to scale it up to casserole level. With its melty Brie and crispy bread crumbs smothered over Brussels sprouts, it's honestly the side that your holiday table has been missing. Or any weeknight table, really.

Serves 6 to 8

2 tablespoons extra-virgin olive oil

3 tablespoons unsalted butter, cut into 3 pieces, plus more for baking dish

2 onions, thinly sliced

2 teaspoons kosher salt, plus more for seasoning

2 pounds (910 g) Brussels sprouts

1 cup (240 ml) heavy cream

2½ cups (250 g) freshly grated Parmesan cheese, plus more for topping

1 teaspoon freshly ground black pepper

Zest and juice of 1 lemon

1 (8-ounce/225 g) wheel firm Brie cheese, cut into ¼-inch (6 mm) strips

1 cup (45 g) fresh bread crumbs

In a large skillet over medium-high heat, pour in the oil and add the butter. Swirl pan until the butter is melted. Reduce heat to medium-low and add the onions. Cook, stirring occasionally, until the onions are caramelized, about 45 minutes, adding 1 tablespoon of water every 15 minutes or so. Season with salt. Set aside to cool.

Preheat the oven to 400°F (205°C). Grease a 9 by 13-inch (23 by 33 cm) baking dish.

Bring a stockpot of salted water to a boil. Prepare an ice water bath. Drop the Brussels into the salted water and boil for 5 minutes, then transfer immediately to the ice water bath to halt cooking. Once cool to the touch, transfer the Brussels to a large kitchen towel and pat well to dry. Slice them in half and transfer to a large bowl.

Add the cream, Parmesan, 2 teaspoons salt, black pepper, and lemon juice and zest. Add the caramelized onions and toss to combine.

Transfer to a prepared baking dish. Top with the slices of Brie, the fresh bread crumbs, and a generous layer of Parmesan.

Transfer to the oven and cook until the liquid is bubbling and the surface is deep golden brown, 20 to 25 minutes. Allow to cool for 10 minutes, then serve.

Al Pastor
Dinner Party

Full menu serves 6

One of the last trips we went on pre-pandemic was to Mexico City, and when I tell you that we ate our weight in tacos, I'm not exaggerating. We paired that with the fact that we walked more than fifteen miles a day discovering new neighborhoods, taking in the sights, and meeting cool makers and shop owners. It was an incredible trip and one that I highly recommend, especially for the food. But in the meantime, this menu will give you a taste of the amazingness that Mexico City has to offer. The highlight is the al pastor-inspired chicken, which borrows its cooking method from the lamb shawarma brought to Mexico by Lebanese immigrants. The meat gets slathered in a traditional chile-and-spice-packed marinade called adobada, then grilled (since I can't exactly have you installing an entire spit to roast the chicken!). And while pineapple plus al pastor is a divisive issue in Mexico, I'm all for that hit of salty and sweet. After this labor of love, you just need to whip together a fun chopped salad that features zucchini and squash, plus a few rounds of tequila cocktails, naturally!

El Sueño

In a cocktail shaker, pour the tequila, orange juice, lime juice, vanilla, honey, and bitters with the salt. Give a good stir to combine the honey and vanilla. Fill the cocktail shaker three-quarters full with ice and shake for 10 seconds. Divide into four glasses and top with a splash of Topo Chico. Garnish with a lime or orange twist.

PREP AHEAD TIP: Make it in bulk and keep it in a pitcher. Add ice before serving and after you pour a glass, top with Topo Chico.

1 cup (240 ml) tequila blanco

1 cup (240 ml) freshly squeezed orange juice

¼ cup (60 ml) freshly squeezed lime juice

2 teaspoons vanilla extract

2 teaspoons honey

3 to 4 dashes bitters

Pinch kosher salt

Lime or orange rind twist for garnish

1 (12-ounce/355 ml) Topo Chico, or your favorite sparkling water

Calabacitas-Style
Chopped Salad
with Cilantro Vinaigrette

1 tablespoon extra-virgin olive oil

1 yellow onion, diced

1 poblano pepper, diced

3 cloves garlic, roughly chopped

1 red bell pepper, diced

1 orange bell pepper, diced

1 zucchini, diced

1 yellow squash, diced

1 cup (135 g) frozen yellow corn

1 (4-ounce/115 g) can green chiles

Kosher salt and freshly cracked
    black pepper

4 to 6 heads of baby romaine, sliced

1 recipe Cilantro Vinaigrette
    (page 235)

In a large cast-iron skillet, heat the oil over medium-high heat. Add the onion and poblano pepper and sauté for 4 to 5 minutes, until the onion is translucent. Add the garlic and stir to combine.

Add the red and orange bell peppers, zucchini, and yellow squash and cook for another 5 minutes, until the zucchini and squash are slightly soft. Stir in the corn and green chiles, season with salt and pepper, and continue to sauté for a few minutes more, until the corn is warmed through. Remove the skillet from the heat and let cool.

Transfer the veggie mixture to the bottom of a large, wide, shallow bowl. Add the romaine on top, and toss with the cilantro vinaigrette when ready to serve.

Al Pastor–Inspired Chicken

TO MAKE THE CHICKEN: In a blender or food processor, blend the garlic cloves, chipotle peppers, orange juice, pineapple juice, vinegar, brown sugar, chile powder, cumin, paprika, granulated garlic, oregano, and salt until smooth.

Transfer the chicken to a zip-top plastic bag and pour in the marinade. Let marinate for at least 4 to 6 hours, but no more than 10.

Preheat an indoor or outdoor grill to medium-high heat. After the chicken has marinated, remove from the liquid to a plate, letting any excess liquid drip off, and season with salt and black pepper.

Transfer to the grill and grill for 6 to 7 minutes per side until cooked through. Remove and let rest for 10 minutes.

TO MAKE THE GUACAMOLE: Cut the avocados in half lengthwise. Remove the pit from the avocado and discard. Remove the avocado from the skin and place the avocado flesh into a bowl. Add the lemon juice, lime juice, red onion, chives, jalapeño, salt and pepper. Mash with a fork until half smooth and creamy. Taste and add more salt and pepper if desired

TO SERVE: Thinly slice the meat against the grain and serve alongside the tortillas, salsas, onions, cilantro, pineapple, and guacamole.

FOR THE CHICKEN:

3 cloves garlic

2 to 3 chipotle peppers, from a can packed in adobo sauce

¾ cup (180 ml) freshly squeezed orange juice

¾ cup (180 ml) freshly juiced pineapple juice

1 tablespoon apple cider vinegar

2 tablespoons brown sugar, honey, or agave

1 tablespoon ancho chile powder

1 teaspoon ground cumin

1 teaspoon paprika

1 teaspoon granulated garlic

1 teaspoon dried oregano

1½ teaspoons kosher salt

12 boneless, skinless chicken thighs (about 3.5 pounds)

FOR THE GUACAMOLE:

4 ripe Hass avocados

⅓ cup (40 g) finely chopped red onion

3 tablespoons freshly chopped chives

Juice of ½ lemon

Juice of ½ lime

2 teaspoons finely chopped jalapeño

Kosher salt and freshly cracked black pepper

FOR SERVING:

Charred flour and/or corn tortillas

Tomatillo Salsa (page 233)

Chipotle Salsa (page 234)

Chopped yellow onions

Fresh cilantro

Grilled pineapple, cut into small dice

Cinnamon Ice Cream Trifle with Mexican Wedding Cookies + Cajeta *Mixed with Whipped Cream*

FOR THE CINNAMON ICE CREAM:

2 cups (480 ml) heavy cream

1 cup (240 ml) whole milk

⅔ cup (145 g) packed brown sugar

1 teaspoon ground cinnamon

Pinch kosher salt

1 teaspoon vanilla extract

5 large egg yolks

FOR THE DULCE DE LECHE WHIPPED CREAM:

2 cups (480 ml) heavy whipping cream, chilled

½ cup (65 g) confectioners' sugar

2 teaspoons vanilla extract

½ cup (120 ml) store-bought dulce de leche

FOR THE MEXICAN WEDDING COOKIES:

1 cup (2 sticks/225 g) unsalted butter

½ cup 100 g) granulated sugar

2 teaspoons vanilla extract

2 cups (480 ml) all-purpose flour

1 cup (95 g) finely chopped almonds, plus more for serving

½ cup (65 g) confectioners' sugar

TO MAKE THE ICE CREAM: In a medium saucepan over medium heat, whisk together the heavy cream, milk, brown sugar, cinnamon, and salt. Bring just to a simmer, stir, then remove from the heat. Stir in the vanilla.

In a medium bowl, whisk together the yolks. Stirring constantly, add about ½ cup (120 ml) of the hot liquid to the egg yolks. This helps to temper them, cooking them super slowly and bringing the temperature up gradually. Whisk in another ½ cup (120 ml) of the hot liquid, and then one more ½ cup (120 ml).

Pour the egg mixture back into the saucepan and cook over medium heat until the mixture is thick enough to coat the back of a spoon.

Scrape the mixture into a container and cover. Chill for at least 4 hours or overnight.

Add the chilled base to the canister of your ice cream churn and churn according to manufacturer's instructions. Once done, freeze for a few hours until ready to serve.

TO MAKE THE WHIPPED CREAM: In the chilled bowl of a stand mixer, combine the whipping cream, confectioners' sugar, and vanilla. Starting on low speed and increasing to medium high, whip until the cream forms soft peaks. Add the dulce de leche and continue to whip until semifirm peaks form. Cover and place in the fridge until ready to use.

TO MAKE THE MEXICAN WEDDING COOKIES: In a medium bowl, cream the butter and granulated sugar. Stir in vanilla and 2 teaspoons water. Add the flour and almonds, and mix until blended. Cover and chill for 3 hours.

Preheat the oven to 325°F (165°C). Shape the dough into balls. Place on an unprepared cookie sheet and bake for 15 to 20 minutes. Transfer the cookies to wire racks to cool. When cookies are cool, roll in confectioners' sugar. Store at room temperature in an airtight container.

TO ASSEMBLE: Scoop the ice cream into a glass or single-serving bowl. Top with a few Mexican wedding cookies broken in half or whole and a big spoonful of the whipped cream. Garnish with extra crushed or chopped almonds if desired.

Decadent Things

When it comes to dessert, I say the more the merrier. Bring on the creamy, the sugary, the dense, and the whipped. Cookies, cakes, ice cream—the works. You could definitely say that dessert is my love language, which pretty much means that I'll stop at nothing to make sure that I can get a fix as quickly and as easily as possible. Enter these recipes, which will ensure that you end up with all the decadence and none of the hassle, and that you'll look like a total rock star presenting the finished product.

Page 204:
Chocolate
Nutella Pie

Adam's Nutella Slablova with Freeze-Dried Strawberries

By now you all know that Adam is a magician when it comes to recipes. Well, let me just tell you that he has completely outdone himself with this "slablova," the nickname we gave the dessert because it's a Pavlova in the shape of a slab. He brought it to the pool one day, and everyone's minds were blown by how beautiful the pavlova looked, all swirled with cocoa powder. And then there was the luscious sour cream and Nutella topping. It's seriously next-level—and yet you don't have to be a culinary magician to make it.

Serves 8+

FOR THE MERINGUE:

1½ cups (295 g) superfine sugar
½ cup (65 g) powdered sugar
9 egg whites, at room temperature
Pinch of kosher salt
¼ teaspoon cream of tartar
1 teaspoon vanilla extract
1 teaspoon white vinegar
⅓ cup (30 g) cocoa powder
¼ cup (30 g) crushed pistachios, plus more for garnish
¼ cup (35 g) crushed freeze-dried strawberries, plus more for garnish
1 pint (290 g) strawberries, cleaned, hulled, and cut in half
1 cup (125 g) raspberries
2 tablespoons granulated sugar

FOR THE WHIPPED CREAM:

2 cups (480 ml) Nutella
2 cups (480 ml) sour cream
2 cups (480 ml) heavy whipping cream, chilled
½ cup (65 g) powdered sugar
2 teaspoons vanilla extract

TO MAKE THE MERINGUE: Heat oven to 230°F (110°C).

Line a sheet pan with parchment paper. Use a pencil to draw an 8 by 11-inch (20 cm by 28 cm) rectangle on the parchment then flip over.

Combine the superfine sugar with the powdered sugar and set aside.

In the clean bowl of a stand mixer, combine the egg whites, salt, and cream of tartar. Start beating on low then gradually increase speed to high once you see a nice froth starting, about 2 minutes. Continue beating on high until you have nice, firm peaks, then begin adding the sugar mixture 1 heaping tablespoon at a time. Continue beating until stiff and shiny. This should take 8 to 10 minutes.

Add the vanilla and vinegar and continue to beat for 1 more minute. Turn off the mixer and remove the bowl from the stand. Test to make sure you feel no small granules of sugar by rubbing the mixture between your fingers. If you feel something gritty, continue mixing until it's smooth.

Secure the parchment to the sheet pan by placing a small amount of meringue under each of the four corners of the parchment. Use a sieve to sprinkle half of the cocoa powder over the meringue in the bowl, then use a large spoon to swirl to combine, but don't overmix. You want it to be streaky.

With the same spoon, scoop up large mounds of meringue and place them on the parchment. Once the top layer of meringue is used, repeat swirling with more cocoa powder and scooping onto the parchment until you've filled in the pencil-drawn outline.

(continued)

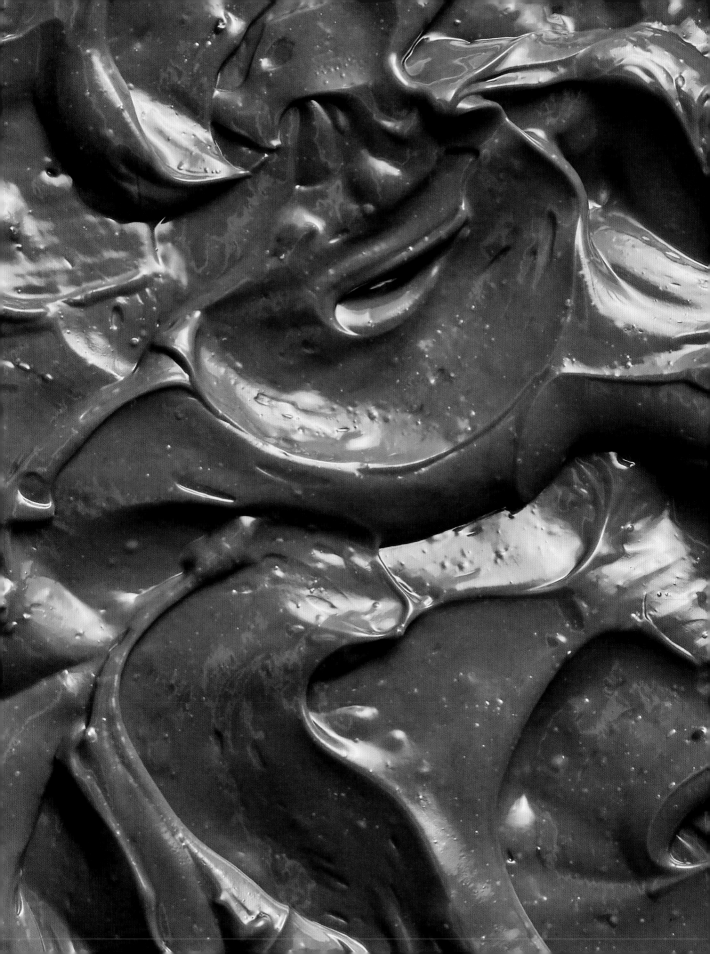

Use the spoon to smooth out the center of the slablova and place it in the oven for 2 hours or until it's firm and set. It will puff slightly as it cooks. Turn the oven off, slide the slablova carefully out of the oven, and sprinkle on the pistachios and freeze-dried strawberries. Return to the oven, close the door, and allow to cool for 3 to 4 hours or overnight.

In a medium bowl, mix the berries and granulated sugar and place in the fridge.

TO MAKE THE WHIPPED CREAM: In a medium bowl, mix the Nutella and sour cream, stirring with a spoon until combined. Remove ½ cup (120 ml) to be added to the whipped cream, cover, and place the remaining mixture in the fridge until ready to use.

In the chilled bowl of a stand mixer, combine the heavy cream, powdered sugar, and vanilla. Start mixing on low, gradually increasing the speed to medium-high until the cream is at soft peaks. Add the reserved Nutella mixture and continue to whip until semi-firm peaks form. Cover and place in the fridge until ready to use.

TO ASSEMBLE: Remove the slablova from the sheet pan and spoon the Nutella on the top, followed by the whipped cream and berries. Toss on some extra pistachios and freeze-dried strawberries and serve large spoonfuls in bowls.

Upside-Down Peach Cake

Skillet

I have a peach farmer friend (shout out to Tenerelli Orchards!) here in L.A. who grows insanely perfect peaches during peach season. As a result, I put them in everything—every salad, every salsa, every batch of food for Poppy. And now they're being showcased in this upside-down cake, which is extraordinary. The cornmeal in the batter gives the whole thing a bit more bite and also complements the sweetness of the peaches, which—don't worry—don't have to come from a friend's orchard to be perfectly delicious.

Serves 8-plus

3 medium peaches, cut into ⅓-inch (8 mm) wedges
1 tablespoon fresh lemon juice
¾ cup (95 g) all-purpose flour
½ cup (60 g) coarse cornmeal
¾ teaspoon baking powder
¼ teaspoon baking soda
1 teaspoon salt
2 teaspoons ground cinnamon
½ cup (115 g/1 stick) plus 3 tablespoons unsalted butter, at room temperature
½ cup (100 g) plus ¼ cup (50 g) granulated sugar
½ cup (110 g) packed brown sugar
2 large eggs, at room temperature
1 tablespoon vanilla bean paste
½ cup (120 ml) sour cream
Vanilla ice cream or whipped cream, for serving

Preheat the oven to 350°F (175°C). Line a rimmed sheet pan with parchment paper.

In a bowl, combine the peaches with the lemon juice. Set aside.

In another bowl, whisk together the flour, cornmeal, baking powder, baking soda, salt, and cinnamon. Set aside.

In a stand mixer fitted with the paddle attachment, beat ½ cup (115 g) of the butter, ½ cup (100 g) of the granulated sugar, and ½ cup (110 g) of the brown sugar until light and fluffy, about 3 minutes. Add the eggs and vanilla bean paste and continue to beat until combined.

In three additions, add the flour mixture, beating until just combined. Then add the sour cream and beat until combined. Set aside.

Place a 10-inch (25 cm) cast-iron skillet over medium heat. Pour in the remaining ¼ cup (50 g) granulated sugar and cook, stirring occasionally, until the sugar melts and turns a dark amber color, about 7 minutes. Add the remaining 3 tablespoons butter and stir until melted and somewhat combined with the sugar.

Arrange the peaches on the bottom of the skillet. Cover the peaches in batter, spreading into an even layer. Place the skillet on the prepared sheet pan. Bake until a toothpick inserted in the center comes out clean, 40 to 45 minutes. Let the cake cool for 15 minutes, then run a knife around the edge to loosen from the pan. Invert out onto a plate. Slice and serve with vanilla ice cream or dollops of whipped cream.

Basque Cheesecake

I'm not usually one to drop the eff bomb (publicly), but this cake is so f*cking good, and I will forever be indebted to my best friend Emily for introducing me to her favorite dessert. It's rich and creamy—exactly as a good cheesecake should be— but what makes it unique is that it's even better served warm. Though, you could also make it a day ahead and serve it chilled. Or leave it out on the counter overnight and eat it the next morning (not that I know anything about that). Salted caramel is optional, but let's be honest—you need it in your life. Emily, this one is for you! Feel free to make it for me anytime.

Preheat the oven to 400°F (205°C). Spray a 9-inch (23 cm) springform pan with nonstick cooking spray, then line with parchment with at least a 3-inch (7.5 cm) overhang on all sides.

In the bowl of a stand mixer fitted with a paddle attachment, beat the cream cheese until smooth, about 1 minute. Add the sugar and continue to beat on medium until no granules of sugar remain and the cream cheese is lump-free, about 2 minutes.

Add the eggs one at a time, beating on medium low in between additions, until combined. Then beat in the vanilla bean paste and salt.

Scrape down the sides of the bowl and add the cream, beating until just combined.

Sift the flour over the cream cheese mixture. Use a rubber spatula to fold the flour into the mixture until cohesive and silky.

Transfer the batter to the prepared pan and place on a rimmed sheet pan. Transfer to the middle rack of the oven and bake until the cheesecake is deeply browned on top (it will almost look burnt but that's cool!), jiggles slightly in the center, and is set on the sides, about 1 hour.

Allow the cheesecake to cool for 40 minutes, then carefully unmold. Peel the parchment away, slice, and serve warm with whipped cream and salted caramel.

Serves 8-plus

4 (8-ounce/226 g) packages cream cheese, at room temperature

1⅓ cups (265 g) granulated sugar

6 large eggs, at room temperature

2 teaspoons vanilla bean paste

1 teaspoon kosher salt

1¾ cups (420 ml) heavy cream, at room temperature

¼ cup (30 g) all-purpose flour

Lightly sweetened whipped cream, for serving

Store-bought salted caramel sauce, for serving (optional)

Gooey
Triple-Chocolate Cookies

If you've ever been torn between making cookies and brownies,
this recipe is for you. The dense chocolate dough with semisweet chunks and
extra chocolate chunks on top, plus a sprinkling of flaky salt, are the things
of your cookie-brownie-mashup dreams. Dad, I made these for you.
And I expect them stocked anytime we come visit!

Makes 14 cookies

2½ cups (350 g) all-purpose flour,
   scooped and leveled
½ cup (50 g) Dutch-process
   cocoa powder
1 teaspoon baking powder
1 teaspoon baking soda
1½ teaspoons kosher salt
1 teaspoon espresso powder
1 cup (225 g/2 sticks) plus
   2 tablespoons unsalted butter,
   at room temperature
¾ cup (150 g) plus 2 tablespoons
   granulated sugar
1 cup (220 g) packed dark
   brown sugar
2 large eggs, at room temperature
1 tablespoon vanilla extract
2 cups (12 ounces/340 g) semisweet
   chocolate, roughly chopped,
   plus ½ cup (4 ounces/85 g)
   more for topping
Flaky salt, for topping

In a bowl, combine the flour, cocoa powder, baking powder, baking soda, salt, and espresso powder.

In the bowl of an electric mixer, beat the butter, granulated sugar, and brown sugar on medium speed until light and fluffy, about 3 minutes, scraping down the sides of the bowl as needed.

Add the eggs, one at a time, beating until incorporated. Add the vanilla and beat to combine.

In three additions, add the flour mixture, beating on low between each addition until no dry streaks remain.

Beat in the chopped chocolate. Cover and chill the dough for 30 minutes.

Preheat the oven to 350°F (175°C). Line two sheet pans with parchment paper. Scoop and roll the dough into 2½-inch (6 cm) balls. Place on the prepared sheet pans, spacing at least 2 inches (5 cm) apart. Top each ball with a piece of the remaining chocolate chunks, pressing down slightly, then sprinkle with flaky salt.

Bake the cookies for 12 minutes, then remove from the oven and lightly bang the tray on the counter to deflate them slightly. Return to the oven and continue to bake until the cookies are set and the chocolate is very melty, 2 to 3 minutes longer.

NOTE: There are a couple different techniques you can use when measuring flour for making cookies. I'm a scoop-and-level kind of girl and highly recommend that you do it that way too—but we put in the weighted measurement in grams to be the most PRECISE.

S'more Pizookie

The What's Gaby Cooking Facebook group is one of my favorite places on the Internet. It's basically a group of humans who love nothing more than eating, cooking, and feeding people—my kind of peeps! When I was originally concepting this book, I asked the group, "What's one dessert that you want but haven't made before?" Well, this one goes out to Lauren, who made the suggestion that spoke to my soul: a pizookie and s'mores mashup. A pizookie, for those of you who haven't yet gotten to enjoy the most important development in baking since birthday cake, is a giant cookie in the shape of a pizza. And after much testing (it's a tough job, I know), we have arrived. And it's perfect.

Preheat the oven to 350°F (175°C).

In a microwave-safe bowl, melt the butter and transfer it into an unheated bowl.

Add the brown sugar and whisk to combine. Add the vanilla and egg and continue to whisk until totally incorporated.

Add the flour, graham cracker crumbs, baking powder, salt, and baking soda to the wet ingredients and stir until fully combined. Add the chocolate chips and marshmallows and stir to combine.

Spray a medium-size skillet with baking spray. Transfer the batter into the skillet and spread it evenly. Bake for 22 to 24 minutes until just still slightly gooey in the middle and golden around the edges. Remove from the oven and let rest for a few minutes before topping with scoops of ice cream and serving. It's 100 percent meant to be eaten right out of the skillet.

Serves 8-plus

½ cup (115 g/1 stick) unsalted butter
1 cup (220 g) dark brown sugar
2 teaspoons vanilla extract
1 large egg
1 cup (125 g) all-purpose flour
¼ cup (30 g) ground graham cracker crumbs
½ teaspoon baking powder
¼ teaspoon kosher salt
⅛ teaspoon baking soda
¾ cup (130 g) semisweet chocolate chips
¾ cup (38 g) mini marshmallows
Vanilla ice cream, for serving

Chocolate Nutella Pie

Behold this epic trio: Oreo crust, Nutella-cream cheese filling, and whipped cream on top. It is insanity in the best possible way, and sweet but not overly sweet. Add some strawberries on top, because it always pays off to be extra.

Serves 8+

FOR THE CRUST:

25 whole chocolate sandwich cookies, such as Oreos

4 tablespoons unsalted butter, melted

FOR THE FILLING:

2 cups (480 ml) heavy cream

1¼ cups (155 g) confectioners' sugar

1 cup (240 ml) Nutella

1 (8-ounce/226 g) package cream cheese, softened

FOR ASSEMBLY:

Baby strawberries

Shaved chocolate or melted chocolate

TO MAKE THE CRUST: Preheat the oven to 350°F (175°C). In a food processor, pulse the cookies until they're fine crumbs. Pour the melted butter over the top and pulse to combine. Press the mixture into a pie pan and bake until set, 5 to 7 minutes. Remove from the oven and allow to cool completely.

TO MAKE THE FILLING: In a medium bowl, whip the heavy cream and confectioners' sugar with a hand mixer until soft peaks form. Divide the mixture in half.

In a large bowl, whip the Nutella with the cream cheese with a hand mixer until smooth. Add in half of the whipped cream and beat until smooth, scraping the sides as needed.

Pour the filling into the crust, evening out the top with a knife or spatula. Chill for at least an hour before serving.

FOR ASSEMBLY: Top with dollops of the reserved whipped cream, the strawberries, and the chocolate shavings. Serve as needed.

Ice Cream

At some point at the height of COVID-19 quarantine (and my pregnancy),
I whipped up some ice cream recipes and went to TOWN. I don't think
I'd made ice cream since I was in pastry school, but it definitely seemed like
the time to revisit it, and that was definitely one of my better decisions.
After playing around with a ton of flavor experiments, I landed on this one:
a mascarpone-base with all the mix-ins of tiramisu. It might be—besides
Poppy—one of the best things to come out of the craziness of the past couple
years. And the best part? No ice cream machine required.

Put a 9 by 3 by 5-inch (23 by 7.5 by 12 cm) loaf pan in the freezer.

TO MAKE THE ICE CREAM BASE: Combine the mascarpone cheese, condensed milk, espresso powder, vanilla, and salt in a large bowl. Stir to combine.

In a medium bowl, whip the heavy cream with a hand mixer on medium-high speed until firm peaks form. Fold in the mascarpone mixture with the whipped cream until well blended. Pour the mixture into the chilled pan and freeze, covered, until it's almost set, about 2 hours.

TO ADD THE MIX-INS: Remove the mascarpone mixture from the freezer and swirl in the crushed lady fingers, mini chocolate chips, and cocoa powder with a spoon. Return to the freezer until solid, 4 to 5 hours. Serve as needed.

Serves 6 to 8

FOR THE ICE CREAM BASE:
1 cup (225 g) mascarpone cheese,
   at room temperature
1 (14-ounce/420 ml) can sweetened
   condensed milk
2 teaspoons espresso powder
2 teaspoon vanilla extract
Pinch kosher salt
2 cups (480 ml) heavy cream, cold

FOR THE MIX-INS:
½ cup (60 g) crushed
   lady finger cookies
¼ cup (1½ ounces/45 g)
   mini chocolate chips
4 tablespoons Dutch-process
   cocoa powder

Spoon Cake

Want to know why it's called a spoon cake? Because the soft, custardy,
vanilla-scented cake is meant to be spooned . . . directly into your mouth.
This recipe is perfect for swirling with your favorite seasonal fruit,
from fall figs to spring strawberries to summer cherries.

Serves 6 to 8

8 ounces (225 g) fresh seasonal fruit,
  such as berries, pitted cherries,
  sliced pears, pitted and sliced
  stone fruit, or halved figs
¼ cup (50 g) plus ⅓ cup (65 g)
  granulated sugar
1 cup (125 g) all-purpose flour
1 teaspoon baking powder
1 teaspoon kosher salt
1 stick unsalted butter, melted
2 teaspoons vanilla extract
  or bean paste
½ cup (120 ml) milk
Vanilla ice cream, for serving

Preheat the oven to 350°F (175°C). Spray an 8-inch (20 cm) round cake pan with nonstick cooking spray.

In a bowl, combine the fruit and ¼ cup (50 g) of the sugar. Set aside.

In a medium bowl, combine the flour, baking powder, and salt.

In another bowl, combine the melted butter, remaining ⅓ cup sugar, vanilla, and milk. Add the dry ingredients and stir until no streaks of batter remain. Transfer to the prepared pan.

Add the fruit and its accumulated juices, distributing it evenly on the batter.

Bake on the middle rack of the oven until a toothpick comes out clean, about 25 minutes.

Serve with vanilla ice cream.

Lemon-Berry *Easy* "Pudding"

Okay, so it's not technically a pudding, but this cake is luscious, creamy, and pudding-like in all the right ways. It has a bright, fresh lemon flavor that's basically begging for berries and a big dollop of lightly sweetened whipped cream.

Divide the berries evenly between eight 4-ounce (115 g) jars or ramekins. Place on a rimmed sheet pan.

In a medium saucepan over medium heat, combine the cream, sugar, and salt. Bring to a boil for 5 minutes, watching carefully, as it can easily over-boil and spill out of the pot. Whisk occasionally until the sugar is dissolved. Remove from heat and whisk in the lemon juice and vanilla bean paste.

Divide evenly between the prepared jars or ramekins. Refrigerate for at least 5 hours or up to overnight.

Top with the whipped cream and reserved berries to serve.

Serves 8

- 1½ cups (220 g) fresh berries, such as raspberries, blueberries, or sliced strawberries, plus more for topping
- 2½ cups (600 ml) heavy cream
- ¼ cup (50 g) plus 2 tablespoons granulated sugar
- ¼ teaspoon kosher salt
- ¼ cup (60 ml) fresh lemon juice
- 2 teaspoons vanilla bean paste
- Lightly sweetened whipped cream, for serving

Blueberry
Muffin Cookies

Here I've taken my favorite base recipe for a cookie and added a hint of cinnamon, white chocolate chips, and dried blueberries. The effect is like if a cookie and a blueberry muffin got married and had babies. As you can imagine: a must-bake.

Makes about 24 cookies

FOR THE COOKIES:

2¼ cups (330 g) all-purpose flour, scooped and leveled

1 teaspoon baking soda

1½ teaspoons kosher salt

2½ teaspoons ground cinnamon

1 cup (225 g/2 sticks) unsalted butter, at room temperature

1 cup (220 g) packed brown sugar

½ cup (100g) granulated sugar

2 large eggs, at room temperature

2 teaspoons vanilla extract

1 cup (130 g) dried blueberries

2 cups (330 g) white chocolate chips

FOR THE TOPPING:

1 cup (165 g) white chocolate chips

2 teaspoons canola oil

½ cup (65 g) dried blueberries

Demerara sugar, for sprinkling

TO MAKE THE COOKIES: In a medium bowl, whisk together the flour, baking soda, kosher salt, and cinnamon.

In a stand mixer fitted with a paddle attachment, cream the butter, brown sugar, and granulated sugar together until light and fluffy, about 3 minutes. Add the eggs and vanilla, making sure to scrape down the sides of the mixing bowl. Add the flour, baking soda, salt, and cinnamon mixture and mix on low speed until everything is incorporated.

Fold in the blueberries and white chocolate chips.

Cover the bowl and chill the dough for 2 hours.

Line two sheet pans with parchment paper. Preheat your oven to 350°F (175°C).

For each cookie, scoop out 2 tablespoons of dough, roll into a ball, and place on the prepared sheet pan, spacing each scoop at least 2-inches (5 cm) apart. Transfer to the oven and bake until golden brown, 12 to 14 minutes.

Remove from the oven and allow to cool for 4 minutes on the sheet pan, then transfer to a wire rack to cool completely.

TO MAKE THE TOPPING: In a microwave-safe bowl, pour in the white chocolate chips. Microwave in 15-second increments until melted. Add the canola oil and stir until smooth. Transfer to a plastic bag or pastry bag, then snip off a very small bit of the corner or tip. Drizzle the cookies with white chocolate, then strategically place blueberries on the white chocolate so they adhere. Sprinkle cookies with Demerara sugar. Allow to harden, about 1 hour.

NOTE: There are a couple of different techniques you can use when measuring flour for making cookies. I'm a scoop-and-level kind of girl and highly recommend that you do it that way too.

Spring Roll Party

Full menu serves 4

Once upon a time, Matt and Adam had this glorious spring roll party—and I wasn't invited. Apparently you're allowed to have more than one friend! (Not that I'd ever hold a grudge.) Anyway, after seeing some of the photos, I knew that we were going to have to recreate it—it was colorful, bright, fresh, and best of all, everything got cooked tableside with everyone pitching in. How fun is that? There's a little prep work that goes into getting everything set up beforehand and whipping up your dipping sauces, but once everyone gets there, it's all hands on deck to stuff the rice paper wrappers with all the fixings of choice, and then eat as many rolls as humanly possible. The only thing that could make it even more vibrant and fun are some Lemongrass Vodka Spritzes and Minty Lime Sorbet.

Lemongrass
Vodka Spritz

TO MAKE THE SIMPLE SYRUP: In a large saucepan, stir the sugar together with 2 cups (480 ml) water until well-combined. Add the lime juice and zest, lemongrass, ginger, and mint leaves and place over a medium heat. Stir until all of the sugar dissolves. Remove from the heat and leave for a couple of hours to infuse. Strain and decant into sterilized bottles.

TO MAKE THE COCKTAIL: Stir 2 ounces (55 g) of vodka together with ½ to 1 ounce (14 to 28 g) of the simple syrup until combined. Pour into a glass with crushed ice and add ½ cup (120 ml) Topo Chico on top.

FOR THE SIMPLE SYRUP:

2 cups (400 g) granulated sugar

Zest and juice of 3 large limes

2 lemongrass stalks, white part only, halved

4 coin-size slices of ginger

1 big handful mint leaves

FOR THE COCKTAIL:

8 ounces (240 ml) vodka

2 cups (480 ml) Topo Chico, or your favorite sparkling water

Spring Rolls
with Peanut Sauce
+ Nuoc Mam

FOR THE PEANUT SAUCE:

¼ cup (60 ml) peanut butter

⅓ cup (75 ml) hoisin sauce

2 tablespoon rice vinegar

1 teaspoon sesame oil

2 tablespoons sambal

¼ cup (40 g) roasted peanuts,
  finely chopped

FOR THE NUOC MAM:

1 tablespoon granulated sugar

1 tablespoon brown sugar

½ cup (120 ml) fish sauce

1 cup (240 ml) warm water

5 tablespoons fresh lime juice

5 cloves garlic, minced

2 Thai chiles or 1 serrano chile
  (less or more—spice is up to you)

2 teaspoons minced fresh ginger

FOR THE SPRING ROLLS:

1 head red leaf lettuce, washed,
  leaves separated

4 large king oyster mushrooms,
  sliced lengthwise into ¼-inch
  (6 mm) planks

4 Persian cucumbers,
  cut into thin wedges

1 large carrot, cut into matchsticks

4 ounces (115 g) French green beans,
  blanched and cooled

Fresh herbs, such as cilantro, mint,
  Thai basil, perilla, Italian basil,
  and chives

(continued)

TO MAKE THE PEANUT SAUCE: In a bowl, whisk together the peanut butter, hoisin sauce, rice vinegar, sesame oil, and sambal to combine. If you'd like a thinner sauce you can add a tablespoon of water. Reserve a small amount of the peanuts for garnish. Whisk the rest of the peanuts into the sauce. Set aside or cover and refrigerate for several days.

TO MAKE THE NUOC MAM: In a bowl, dissolve the sugars in the warm water, mixing with a fork. Add the remaining ingredients and stir to combine. Set aside or cover and refrigerate for several days.

TO PREP THE SPRING ROLLS: Wash and prep the lettuce, mushrooms, cucumbers, carrot, green beans, and herbs and divide between two platters. This is also a good spot for the cooked and cooled rice noodles.

Divide the raw meats between two platters, one for each side of the table. Cover with plastic wrap and refrigerate until ready to grill.

SET THE TABLE: Place the burner and grill pan in the center of the table with two pairs of tongs for cooking. Each side of the table will get a meat platter, veggie plater, rice papers, and warm water to soften. Each person will get two small sauce bowls for the dipping sauces, a set of chopsticks, and a dinner plate. Rice papers are just over 8 inches (20 cm), so 9 to 10-inch (23 to 25 cm) dinner plates work perfectly.

LET'S GET COOKING: Turn the burner on medium-high and let the guests have at it. This is DIY cooking at its best. Encourage each person to get creative with the meat and veggie combinations. A tip: After cooking the pork belly you should have a puddle of delicious pork fat you can use to cook the king oyster mushrooms in AND IT IS HEAVENLY! Oh, and don't forget to grill the pineapple—it's next level.

(continued)

Roll it up! Now that you have a small pile of grilled deliciousness on your plate, quickly dip (see Pro Tip) and roll the rice paper wrapper in the warm water. Lay it flat on the plate; fill with lettuce, herbs, veggies, and meats; and roll up like a burrito. OR for a much prettier presentation, after soaking the rice paper fold it in half, lay it on the plate, layer on the fixings, and roll it up like a cigar, letting all the pretty ingredients spill out of the ends.

PRO TIP: DON'T oversoak the wrappers; they should still be slightly firm when rolling.

1 pound (455 g) rice vermicelli noodles, cooked according to package directions and cooled

20 (8-inch/20 cm) round rice paper wrappers

1 pound (455 g) thin-sliced beef

1 pound (455 g) thin-sliced pork belly

1 pound (455 g) large shrimp, peeled and deveined

8 ounces (225 g) imitation crab

½ small pineapple, peeled, cored, and cut into 4 by ½-inch (10 cm by 12 mm) strips

SPECIAL EQUIPMENT:

Portable tabletop burner (We use one sold in Korean markets for KBBQ.)

Nonstick grill pan

2 rice paper/egg roll water bowl holders (Or you can easily just use 2 medium bowls of warm water on either end of the table.)

4 serving platters

8 small sauce bowls

4 pairs of chopsticks

Minty
Lime Sorbet

FOR THE SIMPLE SYRUP:

2 cups (400 g) granulated sugar

1 stalk lemongrass,
  split down the middle

1 big handful of fresh mint leaves

FOR THE SORBET:

1 cup (240 ml) freshly squeezed
  lime juice

TO MAKE THE SIMPLE SYRUP: In a large saucepan, stir the sugar with 2 cups (480 ml) water until well-combined. Add the lemongrass and bring to a boil. stirring until the sugar is melted. Add the mint leaves and let steep for 20 minutes off the burner. Let cool entirely. Remove the mint leaves and lemongrass stalk, and use for the sorbet.

TO MAKE THE SORBET: In a loaf pan or small baking dish, combine the lime juice with the simple syrup and 1 cup (240 ml) water. Freeze overnight. Once fully chilled, scoop the sorbet to serve.

Sauces + Things

In my opinion, it's the condiments that make the meal. They're like the accessories that bring everything together, whether they're light and bright or rich and savory. When done right, they're what make all the other flavors pop and turn a solid dish into an obsession.

The sauces and dressings in this chapter are paired with dishes throughout the book, but you can also make them on their own and mix and match to your heart's delight. I strongly encourage you to make a batch or two and keep them in the fridge for the week, or, for the vinaigrettes, freeze little portions in ice cube trays so that you can break them out when the craving strikes. Either way, do yourself and your meals a favor and get these recipes into your life.

Homemade Ketchup

Makes about 1 cup (235 ml)

2 tablespoons extra-virgin olive oil
1 medium onion, chopped
1 clove garlic, chopped
1 (28-ounce/795 g) can tomato puree
½ cup (110 g) brown sugar
¼ cup (60 ml) apple cider vinegar
1 tablespoon tomato paste
1 chipotle pepper in adobo sauce
1 teaspoon kosher salt
½ teaspoon ground mustard
½ teaspoon ground cayenne pepper
¼ teaspoon allspice
⅛ teaspoon ground cloves

In a pot, heat the oil over medium heat. Sauté the onion in the oil for 5 to 8 minutes, until translucent. Add the garlic and stir for about 30 seconds. Add the tomato puree, brown sugar, vinegar, tomato paste, chipotle in adobo, salt, mustard, cayenne pepper, allspice, and cloves and stir to combine. Increase heat to high and bring to a boil, then reduce heat to low and simmer, stirring occasionally, for 30 to 45 minutes until it is thick like ketchup.

Using an immersion blender, stand blender, or food processor, puree the mixture until smooth.

Taste and adjust salt as needed. Pour the ketchup into a container and seal. It can be refrigerated for up to 1 month.

Herby Buttermilk Ranch

Makes about 1 cup (235 ml)

⅓ cup (75 ml) plus 1 tablespoon sour cream
⅔ cup (165 ml) mayonnaise
½ cup (120 ml) buttermilk
1½ teaspoons granulated garlic
1 teaspoon granulated onion
1 tablespoon finely minced fresh parsley
1 tablespoon finely minced fresh chives
1 tablespoon finely minced fresh dill
Squeeze of fresh lemon
Kosher salt and freshly cracked black pepper

In a medium bowl, mix together all the ingredients until smooth, then season with more salt and pepper, as desired. Store in an airtight container in the refrigerator for up to 1 week.

Honey Lime Vinaigrette

Makes about ¾ cup (175 ml)

¼ cup (60 ml) fresh lime juice
1 tablespoon champagne vinegar
2 tablespoons honey
1 teaspoon granulated sugar
1 small clove garlic, minced
¼ cup (60 ml) extra-virgin olive oil
¼ cup (60 ml) neutral oil
Kosher salt and freshly ground black pepper

In a medium bowl, combine the lime juice, vinegar, honey, sugar, and garlic. In a slow, steady stream, while whisking constantly, pour in the oils until cohesive. Season with salt and pepper.

Calabrian Vinaigrette

Makes about ½ cup (120 ml)

¼ cup (60 ml) red wine vinegar
1 to 2 tablespoons chopped jarred Calabrian chiles
  (depending on desired spice level)
1 clove garlic, minced
6 tablespoons extra-virgin olive oil
Kosher salt and freshly ground black pepper

In a medium bowl, combine the vinegar, Calabrian chiles, and garlic. In a slow steady stream, while whisking constantly, pour in the oil until cohesive. Season with salt and pepper.

Honey Dijon Vinaigrette

Makes about 1 cup (235 ml)

2 teaspoons freshly grated lemon zest
¼ cup (60 ml) fresh lemon juice
2 teaspoons honey
2 teaspoons Dijon mustard
½ cup (120 ml) extra-virgin olive oil
Kosher salt and freshly ground black pepper

In a medium bowl, combine the lemon zest, juice, honey, and Dijon. In a slow steady stream, while whisking constantly, pour in the oil until cohesive, then season with salt and pepper.

Miso Sesame Vinaigrette

Makes about 1 cup (235 ml)

½ cup (120 ml) white miso paste
2 tablespoons plus 1 teaspoon granulated sugar
3 tablespoons seasoned rice wine vinegar
Splash soy sauce
2 tablespoons sesame oil
2 tablespoons white sesame seeds
Pinch white pepper

In a small bowl, whisk together the miso, 3 tablespoons water, the sugar, vinegar, and soy sauce. In a slow steady stream, while whisking constantly, pour in the sesame oil until smooth and creamy, then add the sesame seeds and a pinch white pepper.

Thai-Style Chimichurri

Makes just over 1 cup (235 ml)

3 cloves garlic
2 teaspoons chopped fresh ginger
5 scallions, trimmed and roughly chopped
1 jalapeño or Thai chile pepper, stemmed and halved
1 cup (40 g) tightly packed fresh cilantro leaves
  and tender stems
1 cup (40 g) tightly packed fresh Thai basil leaves
½ cup (25 g) tightly packed fresh mint leaves
3 tablespoons seasoned rice wine vinegar
1 to 4 teaspoons fish sauce
  (I like four, but I'm a fish sauce freak.)
½ cup (120 ml) extra-virgin olive oil
¼ cup (60 ml) neutral oil
Kosher salt and freshly ground black pepper

With a food processor running, put the garlic through the feeding tube to mince. Turn off the machine and add the ginger, scallions, jalapeño, cilantro, basil, mint, vinegar, and fish sauce.

Process until finely minced. Then, with the machine running, slowly pour in the olive and neutral oils until cohesive. Season with salt and black pepper.

Herby Shallot Vinaigrette

Makes about 1 cup (235 ml)

2 shallots, finely chopped
¼ cup (60 ml) plus 3 tablespoons
    white wine vinegar or white balsamic
1 clove garlic, minced
3 tablespoons minced fresh basil
2 tablespoons minced fresh parsley
3 tablespoons minced fresh chives
½ cup (120 ml) extra-virgin olive oil,
    plus more as needed
Kosher salt
Pinch crushed red pepper

In a small bowl, combine the shallots with the vinegar and let sit for 15 minutes. Add the garlic, basil, parsley, and chives. In a slow steady stream, while whisking constantly, pour in the oil until cohesive, then season with salt and crushed red pepper.

Lemon Vinaigrette

Makes about ¾ cup (175 ml)

Juice of 1 lemon
2 tablespoons red wine vinegar
2 cloves garlic, finely chopped
1 shallot, finely chopped
½ cup (60 ml) olive oil
Kosher salt and freshly cracked black pepper

In a medium bowl, whisk together all the ingredients. Taste and adjust salt and pepper as needed.

Romesco Sauce

Makes about 2 cups (480 ml)

1 large dried ancho chile
4 cloves garlic
1½ teaspoons sea salt, plus more if needed
1 cup (145 g) cherry tomatoes
⅔ cup (95 g) almonds, hazelnuts,
    or a combination, roasted
½ cup (115 g) jarred roasted bell peppers, drained
1 tablespoon sherry or red wine vinegar
1½ teaspoons smoked paprika
1 cup (240 ml) extra-virgin olive oil

Put the ancho chile in hot water and let it soak overnight, or pour boiling water over it and cover with plastic wrap until tender, about 10 minutes.

Chop the garlic on a cutting board with the salt. Using the side of a chef's knife, smash the garlic into the salt to make a paste.

Drain the ancho chile. In the bowl of a food processor, combine the ancho, garlic, tomatoes, nuts, roasted bell peppers, vinegar, and paprika and pulse to make a slightly chunky sauce with no large pieces.

With the machine running, slowly drizzle in the oil. Taste and adjust the seasoning with salt if needed. Transfer to a serving bowl. Cover with plastic and set aside if using within 2 hours. The sauce will keep for about 2 weeks in the refrigerator or up to a month in the freezer.

Homemade Bread Crumbs + Croutons

Makes about 1½ cups (355 ml)

2 tablespoons extra-virgin olive oil
1 tablespoon unsalted butter
2 to 4 slices French bread, a few days old,
  torn into very small pieces
  (1½ cups/70 g once torn)
2 cloves garlic, chopped
½ teaspoon kosher salt

TO MAKE BREAD CRUMBS: In a food processor, pulse the bread until it becomes fine crumbs.

TO MAKE CROUTONS: Place a large nonstick skillet over medium heat with the oil and butter. Add the bread and sauté for 3 to 5 minutes, until it starts to turn golden brown. Add the garlic and salt and continue to sauté for 1 to 2 more minutes until fragrant and toasted. Remove from the heat and transfer to a plate lined with a paper towel to drain any excess oil. Use as needed.

Teriyaki Lime Dressing

Makes about ⅓ cup (80 ml)

¼ cup (60 ml) teriyaki sauce
Juice of 1 lime, plus wedges for serving
1 tablespoon light miso
2 teaspoons toasted sesame oil
½ teaspoon kosher salt
½ teaspoon ground cumin

Pour the teriyaki sauce into a small bowl. Add the lime juice, miso, sesame oil, salt, and cumin. Whisk to combine and set aside.

Tomatillo Salsa

Makes about 1 cup (235 ml)

1 pound (455 g) tomatillos, husked, rinsed,
  and halved
½ small yellow onion, roughly chopped
1 green jalapeño, stem removed and roughly chopped
3 cloves garlic, roughly chopped
⅓ cup (15 g) fresh cilantro, chopped
Juice of 2 limes
1 tablespoon kosher salt

Preheat the oven to 425°F (220°C). Arrange the halved tomatillos on a parchment-lined sheet pan and roast until soft and charred, about 20 minutes.

Remove from the oven and cool. Transfer the tomatillos into a blender or food processor with the onion, jalapeño, garlic, cilantro, lime juice, and salt. Blend until smooth. Taste and adjust seasoning with more cilantro, lime juice, or salt according to preference. Store in an airtight container in the refrigerator for up to 5 days.

Pickled Onions

Makes about 2 cups (480 ml)

1 cup (240 ml) apple cider vinegar
1 tablespoon granulated sugar
1½ teaspoons kosher salt
1 red onion, cut in thin slices

In a small bowl, whisk the vinegar, sugar, and salt together with 1 cup (240 ml) water until the sugar and salt dissolve. Place the sliced onions in a jar and pour the vinegar mixture over the top. Let sit at room temperature for 1 hour. Seal the jar and store in the refrigerator for up to 14 days. Drain and serve as needed.

Chipotle Salsa

Makes about 1 to 2 cups (235 to 475 ml)

1 (28-ounce/795 g) can fire-roasted tomatoes
½ yellow onion, chopped (roughly ½ cup/55 g)
2 cloves garlic
½ jalapeño
2 chipotle peppers in adobo,
    plus 1 teaspoon of the adobo sauce
1 teaspoon kosher salt, plus more as desired
½ teaspoon freshly cracked black pepper,
    plus more if desired
½ cup (20 g) tightly packed fresh cilantro
Juice of 1 lime

In a blender or food processor, pulse all the ingredients until everything is evenly blended. Taste and adjust salt and black pepper as needed. Add more chipotle peppers and pulse if you like it extra spicy. Store in an airtight container in the refrigerator for up to 5 days.

Basil Pesto

Makes about ¾ cup (175 ml)

2 cups (80 g) tightly packed fresh basil leaves
2 tablespoons pine nuts
2 cloves garlic
½ cup (50 g) freshly grated Parmesan cheese
¼ teaspoon salt, plus more as desired
⅛ teaspoon freshly ground black pepper,
    plus more as desired
½ cup (120 ml) extra-virgin olive oil

In the bowl of a food processor, combine the basil, garlic, pine nuts, Parmesan, salt, and pepper. With the motor running, add the oil in a slow stream until emulsified. Season with more salt and pepper if needed. Store in an airtight container in the refrigerator for up to 1 week.

Caramelized Onions

About ½ cup (120 ml)

2 tablespoons extra-virgin olive oil
2 yellow onions, finely diced
Kosher salt

In a large skillet, heat the oil over medium-high heat. Add the onions and sauté for 10 to 15 minutes until they start to caramelize. Reduce the heat to medium, add a few tablespoons of water, and continue to caramelize for about 45 minutes, until deeply brown but not burnt. Season with salt and set aside.

Garlic Labneh

Makes about 1 cup (235 ml)

1 cup (240 ml) store-bought labneh
Pinch kosher salt
2 to 3 cloves garlic
½ cup (75 g) feta cheese

In the bowl of a food processor, pulse all ingredients together until smooth. Season with more salt as desired.

Basil Vinaigrette

Makes about ¾ cup (175 ml)

1 shallot, roughly chopped
2 cups (80 g) tightly packed fresh basil leaves
1 clove garlic
½ teaspoon crushed red pepper
½ cup (120 ml) extra-virgin olive oil
2 tablespoons red wine vinegar
1 teaspoon kosher salt, plus more as desired
Freshly cracked black pepper

In a blender, puree the shallot, basil, garlic, crushed red pepper, oil, vinegar, and salt for 1 minute, until very smooth. Season with salt and black pepper and store in the refrigerator for up to 3 days.

Cilantro Vinaigrette

Makes about ¾ cup (175 ml)

1 shallot, roughly chopped
2 cups (80 g) tightly packed fresh cilantro leaves
1 clove garlic
½ teaspoon crushed red pepper
½ cup (120 ml) extra-virgin olive oil
2 tablespoons red wine vinegar
1 teaspoon kosher salt, plus more as desired
Freshly cracked black pepper

In a blender, puree the shallot, cilantro, garlic, crushed red pepper, oil, vinegar, and salt for 1 minute, until very smooth. Season with more salt if needed and black pepper and store in the refrigerator for up to 3 days.

Lemon Shallot Vinaigrette

Makes about ¾ cup (175 ml)

2 shallots, finely chopped
¼ cup (60 ml) plus 3 tablespoons
   white wine vinegar or white balsamic
1 clove garlic, minced
3 tablespoons minced fresh basil
2 tablespoons minced fresh parsley
3 tablespoons minced fresh chives
½ cup (120 ml) extra-virgin olive oil,
   plus more as needed
Kosher salt
Pinch crushed red pepper

In a blender, pulse all ingredients together until smooth. Season with more salt as desired.

Acknowledgments

My WGC Family: As always, these recipes are for you. I can't think of a more rewarding job than helping you make incredible meals in your own kitchens, for your own friends and family. Thank you so much for your enthusiasm and support, even when I wasn't able to see you in person for a stretch. Luckily, our community on social media is like no other—I love our time together!

Matt and Adam: You are the heart and soul of What's Gaby Cooking, and you're the reason why, four books later, I'm still feeling just as revved up as day one. I am truly the luckiest girl in the world to be able to call the most talented photographer and food stylist in the world my best friends. I love you both!

Amy: Thank you for being the prop stylist of my dreams and so effortlessly capturing the essence of WGC. Your eye for style is truly #goals every day of my life.

Holly: Every writer should be so lucky to have an editor like you. You truly make me feel heard, and the way you bring my visions to life is why I'm here writing another book. Here's to many more!

Janis: I don't know where I'd be without you looking out for me every step of the way. Thank you for your support, direction, and, when necessary, your brutal honesty.

Rachel: Once again, you've managed to climb inside my brain and perfectly capture my voice. A million thank-yous for helping me say everything that I want to say.

Belle: Can we just pick up and travel the world together, eat all the food, drink all the drinks, and then come up with the most amazing recipes afterward? This is my life goal, and I will work to find a way to make it possible every single day for the rest of my life. YOU ARE INCREDIBLE.

Mory: You are a recipe testing and developing machine, and this book is better for it!

Sophie, Diana, Wade, Elizabeth, Laura: This process wouldn't be half as good or as fun without you on set. Thank you for your hard work—and for helping me eat all the leftovers!

Kelsey and Brittney: Thank you for helping me look and feel like my best self. Love you!

Kim: You are an angel. You literally figured out my style, with no direction from me whatsoever, just a glance at my Instagram. You are a genius.

To my friends both near and far: I will forever be grateful to you for the inspiration you give me every day. You are the people I live to cook for and eat with, so to say that you give me life is a dramatic understatement. After these past couple years, I'm so excited to have you back at my table.

Mom, Dad, and Anya: Between a global pandemic and having my first baby, these past couple years have shown me how lucky I am to have you in my life—something I'll never take for granted. I am stronger, more grounded, more confident, and more loving because of you, and I'm endlessly grateful for that.

Thomas: I don't know what I did to deserve you, but I'll take it. You are the best partner a girl could ask for, whether it's being the best dad to Poppy, the best business partner, or the best husband. Any way you slice it, I love you.

Poppy: You changed my world in the best possible way. I am so lucky to be your mom; it truly is the best job in the entire world. Everything I do, I do for you! I cannot wait to show you the world and all the incredible people, food, and cultures that come with it!

Index